# The Melungeons

[NOTES ON THE ORIGIN OF A RACE]

REVISED

Bonnie Ball

Illustrations by
Randy Hodge

The Overmountain Press
JOHNSON CITY, TENNESSEE

ISBN 0-932807-74-7
5  6  7  8  9  0

# ACKNOWLEDGMENTS

I am deeply indebted to the following people and publications for much of the data, statistics, theories, and research used in these notes:

James Aswell, a Tennessee historian, for his theories about the Melungeons.

Ralph Clark of East Tennessee State University, for his research.

Mary Conelly, for "The Lumbee Indians," an article she published in the *Baltimore Sun,* October 30, 1966.

Bruce Crawford, of the former *Crawford's Weekly,* Norton, Virginia, for his many astute observations.

Miss Will Allen Dromgoole, for her writings as published in *The Arena,* at Boston in 1891.

Victor Englebert, for his writings as published in *National Geographic,* in 1968.

G.M. French, Jr., an old settler from Cheverly, Maryland, for information he provided in an interview.

Mrs. Eliza M. Heiskell, for her writings as published in the *Arkansas Gazette* in 1912.

Woodson Knight, for his columns in the *Louisville Courier Journal,* in 1940.

Hampton Osborne, Clintwood, Virginia (a native of Blackwater Valley, Lee County, Virginia), for information he provided in an interview.

H.J. Pearce, Jr., of Emory University, for his writings published in the *Washington Times Herald,* in 1939.

Bill Rawlins, Knoxville, Tennessee, for information as noted on these pages.

Judge Lewis Shepherd, for "A Romantic Account of the Celebrated Melungeon Case," an article he published in the *Chattanooga Times,* in 1914.

Delmer Wallen, Kingsport, Tennessee (a native of Hancock County, Tennessee), for information he graciously provided.

Dr. Goodridge A. Wilson, for "The Southwest Corner," an article he published in the *Roanoke Times* in 1934.

This book is dedicated to those mentioned above, and to all the others whose research, interest, and encouragement enabled me to pursue this most absorbing and fascinating subject.

# INTRODUCTION

Two generations ago, people traveling through certain ranges of the Cumberlands might meet or overtake a group of mountaineers trudging along single-file, making their way to homes concealed in remote hollows and glens. They *were* mountaineers, but there was a difference between them and their white neighbors. They little resembled the Anglo-Saxons, the Scotch-Irish, the Germans, or even the so-called "black Dutch"; and they were entirely unlike the Slavic immigrants seen around regional coal-mining towns. They were dark-skinned, but little about them resembled Italians or Mexicans. Who, then, were they?

Native whites called them "Melungeons." In some ways they reminded people of certain Indian tribes, yet they had other characteristics that suggested a mixture of many races. For example, some of them had the dark skin and curly hair typical of blacks, but even so seldom possessed black facial features. Many writers have described them as a clannish race of people that inhabit the Cumberlands and whose origin lies shrouded in the haze of an uncertain past.

The fact that individual members of these groups have such a wide variation of physical characteristics has given rise to numerous theories concerning their origin. I have known Melungeons since early childhood, when they came from coal towns in adjoining counties to clear land and sharecrop on my father's farm in Lee County, Virginia. Their children attended our public schools, and in later years some of them were my pupils.

My parents knew older Melungeons who lived on Newman's Ridge, along the Virginia-Tennessee border. Their skin was dark and oily, showing more of a coppery color than of, say, Ethiopians or darker members of the white race. Their hair was often coarse and black, and in some families extremely kinked. Others were little different from their white neighbors, with brown or black wavy hair, gray or blue eyes, and rather high, cheekbones. I even recall another type among the Melungeons: those with dark, slightly curly hair, smooth dark skin, and dreamy eyes that seemed almost Oriental.

Some years ago a man named Bill Rawlins, a feature writer from Hancock County, Tennessee, published an article in the *Knoxville News-*

*Sentinel* (October 10, 1958) entitled "East Tennessee Melungeons Have a Past Clouded in Myth." In it, he said:

"The legend of the Melungeons (and for the most part it is legend) goes back nearly three hundred years. Before the year 1700 French explorers reported finding men, not Indians but white men, in the mountain pockets of what is now east Tennessee. One theory of their origin is that a band of ship-wrecked Portuguese sailors wandered from the North Carolina coast into the hills of east Tennessee, married Cherokee Indian maidens, and lived undisturbed until the white man drove them westward. History does not record that Portugal, after revolting successfully against Spain, dispatched a ship to seize Cuba in 1685. No one ever heard from this ship again.

"The census of 1795 listed 300 'free persons' in the mountains of east Tennessee. These apparently were the Melungeons. Whence they came nobody knows. Their origin is as much lost in the recesses of history as their present status is hidden behind the closed-mouth secrecy of Hancock County today. One thing seems certain—they were part Indian. Another seems apparent—they are disappearing the same way they appeared: by marrying others than their own."

Mr. Rawlins gave no authority for any of his comments.

Two decades ago one of the ethnological students of the Cumberlands was Mr. Bruce Crawford, then the publisher of *Crawford's Weekly* (later the *Coalfield Progress)* at Norton in Wise County, Virginia. His research yielded some interesting facts and theories concerning the Melungeons. He found that during their early history both the Carolinas denied the Melungeons the privileges usually accorded to whites. Due to this, many of them migrated to Tennessee. However, two counties in Tennessee ruled that they were black, even though the older Melungeons always claimed positively that they were Portuguese.

In 1887, Tennessee gave Melungeons a separate legal existence, and officially recognized them under the title of "Croatan Indians." The authority for this seems to have been the theory that they were descendants of Sir Walter Raleigh's "Lost Colony," which disappeared from Roanoke Island, North Carolina, about two decades before the English finally established a permanent settlement in America, at Jamestown, Virginia.

As you will recall, Virginia Dare, the first English child born in the New World, was born on Roanoke Island; she was the granddaughter of the colony's governor, John White, who found it necessary to return to England for food and supplies. Due to the war then raging with Spain, Governor White was unable to leave England, and two years passed before he again reached Roanoke Island only to find the settlers missing and the place abandoned. The major clue to their disappearance was the word "CROATOAN" carved on a post of a fort that had been constructed in their absence. This led the governor and his party to conclude that the colonists had been taken captive by an unfriendly tribe, or had gone with the Croatoans for protection and to avoid starvation. Governor White and his party went back to England, leaving the mystery unsolved.

Mr. Rawlins has stated that:

"More romantic is the theory that the Lost Colony, beset by wilderness hardships, moved west, settled with the Indians, and became the forebears of the Melungeons. Adding weight to this theory is the recorded fact that the Melungeons, from their earliest discovery, have spoken an English Dialect. Some of their most common family names are Collins, Mullins, Gibson and Grogan, all of which seem to be English.

"More likely than any of these theories, however, is the possibility that Cherokee Indians married with Europeans who came to this country in more conventional ways—that is, as settlers and explorers. Settling in the mountains, they became isolated from the rest of the world (as Hancock County has remained, to a large extent, to this day); and when they were discovered by the French, they became "Melungeons," the word coming from the French *Melange,* meaning *mixture."*

"Melungeons" in Tennessee, "half-breeds" on the frontier—all of them were part Indian and part white.

In Tennessee, history was to take a different course, partly from a combination of circumstances arising from the overwhelming Scotch-Irish and English ancestry of the settlers, and partly over the slave question. Among the Anglo-Saxons of east Tennessee, a Melungeon was noticed, for if an area were race-conscious already, those of a different race stood out even more. Couple this with a powerful motivator, greed, and you have the situation as it existed in the 1830s. Why greed? For a very specific reason. The Tennessee Constitutional Convention of 1834 succeeded in declaring the Melungeons "free persons *of color*" (italics added), and this changed their legal status. Where they had once been "free persons," they were now "of color," two words which deprived them of their right to hold property, to vote, and even to sue in court. White settlers of the state proceeded to move onto their lands, and the Melungeons headed for the hills to became a band of marauders.

The theory that the Melungeons were possible descendants of the "Lost Colony" and the Croatan Indians has been previously accredited by some ethnologists. Another conjecture is that they were a mixture resulting from a tumultuous period of frontier warfare involving the white captive, the slave, and the Indian captor.

Another theory, widely accepted in the Cumberlands, centers around stories recorded by local historians saying that Hernando de Soto, in his exploration of the Southeast, penetrated a corner of east Tennessee and southwest Virginia during the sixteenth century. Some believe that the Melungeons may have descended from members of his party, lost or captured by the Indians. It *is* true that Melungeons once inhabited Scott and Lee Counties of Virginia in fairly large numbers, forming a teeming colony on Newman's Ridge, which lies along the edges of Scott and Lee Counties in Virginia, and Hancock County in Tennessee.

According to Mr. Crawford, there is another authentic clue as to the origin of the Melungeons. When John Sevier organized the State of Franklin (later Tennessee), a colony of "dark-skinned, reddish-brown complexioned people" already existed. They were supposed to be "of Moorish descent, were neither Indian or black but claimed to be Portuguese. This leads to the most fascinating theory of all—that the Melungeons may have been pure-blooded Carthagenians."

Further research, Mr. Crawford says, yielded traditions that Melungeons descended from the ancient Phoenicians, who migrated from

Carthage to Morroco, crossed the Strait of Gibraltar, and settled in northern Portugal. A colony of these Moors is believed to have crossed the Atlantic before the American Revolution, settling in North Carolina. While the last few paragraphs have been given largely to theories drawn from a few facts and statistics, it is significant that the Moors of Tennessee called themselves Portuguese, or "Porty-gee." However, there are those English surnames again—Gibson, Collins, Sexton, Goins, Mullins, Bowling, etc., and they hardly suggest such an exotic background. While it is possible that the Melungeons, like the slaves and some American Indians, may have adopted such surnames for convenience, it is unlikely that they would or could have adopted English as a language. As previously stated, the word "Melungeon" is one of mystery. While many believe it came from the French word *melange*, others have suggested an origin from *melas*, a Greek word meaning *dark*.

The August, 1959, issue of the *Tennessee Conservationist* contains an article entitled "Melungeons—The Mystery People of Tennessee." In it, some romanticist compares the dark-skinned Melungeons to Othello, who was immortalized by Shakespeare in *Othello, the Moor of Venice.* In another place, the article notes that some people believe the Melungeons descended from the Welsh, who allegedly constructed an old fort near Manchester, Tennessee. This happened (supposedly) long before Christopher Columbus discovered America. The article adds that there are several references in early Americana to "Welsh Indians," who could have been Melungeon forerunners.

Whatever the case, I will attempt to explore as many of these possibilities as I can within the pages of this book. The initial question on the minds of those who have seen and observed the Melungeons seems to be: Who are they? Where did they *really* come from? Other questions follow:

1. Do they have English ancestry? Are they descended from the Lost Colony?
2. Do they have Indian ancestors? If so, what tribes?
3. Is there a connection with the "Lumbee" Indians?
4. Is there a relationship to the Blue Ridge and Piedmont tribes?
5. Is there a Portuguese ancestry?
6. Did De Soto's party have any connection with the Melungeons?
7. What role did slaves play in the evolution of the Melungeons?

8. From whom did they inherit their endurance to hardy, outdoor living? Their superstitions? Their dialects?

9. Why is their history so vague? Why is it so difficult to enumerate them, and give statistics?

10. Are there other kindred people, and if so, where are they?

# CONTENTS

# Chapter One
## THE LOST COLONY

There exists, somewhere, an old Tennessee history that describes in detail an expedition down the Tennessee River in the 1600s. It also records an Indian story of a white settlement eight days down the river, whose people lived in houses and had a large bell. When this bell rang, the people paused and bowed toward it, an act which would suggest a Latin connection. Some believe this settlement might have contained descendants of the Lost Colony, but no concrete evidence has been found which would support this theory.

Another legend says that before 1700, French explorers reported finding men—not Indians, but not wholly white—in the mountain pockets of what is now east Tennessee. They believed these people to have been descendants of a band of ship-wrecked Portuguese sailors who wandered into the hills and met Cherokee women, where they lived undisturbed until white settlers drove them westward.

Other plausible stories name the Moors of Morocco, the Berbers of the Sahara, the Moslem Rifs, the Guineas, the Celts and so on as possible Melungeon ancestors. Theories abound, and one of my objectives in writing this book is to try to discuss as many of them as I can, leaving you free to form your own opinion. But first, my favorite possibility: the Croatoan (or Croatan) Indians and the Lost Colony....

Most writers and historians have discredited the theory that there could have been any connection between the Lost Colony and the Melungeons; and frankly, I did too, for a time. However, more study has convinced me that there probably was a connection. History shows that while the Lost Colony was definitely white, the comments I have italicized on the following pages render it quite possible that other nationalities and races entered the ethnological picture.

### EARLY EXPLORATIONS

During the initial phases of the exploration of North America, Spain and Portugal claimed all the soil as far north as the 44th degree of north latitude (a line crossing southern Maine, central New Hampshire, central

Vermont, northern New York and then west across the Great Lakes). Had their claims prevailed, only the cold regions of the North American continent would have been left for other European countries.

When Henry VIII became King of England in 1509, England broke relations with both Spain and the Roman Catholic Church. Then, under Edward VI (a child king), the claims of Spain to America were disregarded, and a company was formed to promote colonization.

When Queen Mary succeeded Edward VI in 1553 she reestablished Catholicism in England, and enterprises to America were restricted by her and her Spanish husband, Phillip II, to regions of the north, northeast, and northwest, in order to avoid difficulties with Phillip's native land. Then for nearly a century Spain and England grappled for possession of the New World.

Numerous English voyages were made to North America between 1562 and 1600. Conway Whittle Sams, in his *Conquest of Virginia* (Library of Congress, 1924) names the following:

Captain George Ribault, 1562
Captain Thomas Stukey, 1563
Captain John Hawkins, 1562, 1563, and 1567
Sir Martin Frobisher, 1576-77, and 1578
Sir Humphrey Gilbert, 1583
Sir Frances Drake, the first Englishman to sail around the world and make war on the Spaniards, 1580
Sir Humphrey Gilbert, who took possession of Newfoundland, 1583

Sir Walter Raleigh's first expedition to the New World sailed on April 27, 1584, for that part of America he called upon his return "Virginia." According to Sams, Captain Edward Barlow of yet another expedition (1587) gave the following description of the native Americans with whom he came in contact:

"They were of color Yellowish, and their hair black for the most part, and yet *we saw children that had very fine auburn and chestnut-colored hair.*"

These children were assumed by Captain Barlow to have been descendants of sailors who had been shipwrecked on the coast some years earlier, as Sams discusses in later paragraphs.

Barlow continued:

"Within the place where they feed was their lodging, and within that their idol, which they worship, at whom they speak incredible things...when they go to war they carry about with them their idol, the God O-kee, of whom they ask council.

"Toward the southwest [from the viewpoint of Roanoke Island], four days journey, is situated a town called Se-quo-tan [probably Secota in Beaufort County, North Carolina, at the confluence of the Pamlico and Pango Rivers] near which six and twenty years past, there was a ship cast away, *whereof some of the people were saved, and these were white people whom the country people preserved.*

"And after ten days remaining in an out island, uninhabited, called Wo-co-kon, they, with the help of some of the dwellers of Se-quo-tan, fastened two boats of the country together, made masts unto them, and sails of their shirts, and having taken into them such victuals as the country yielded, they departed *after they had remained in this out island three weeks;* but soon afterward it appeared that they were cast away, for the boats were found upon the coast, cast a-land in another island adjoining.

"Other than these, no other white people had been seen among them. They were seen only by inhabitants of Se-co-tan."

The ship mentioned here by Captain Barlow was probably wrecked on the coast of "South Wo-ko-kon." Some of the inhabitants of "Se-co-ta" may have found them there, but the Indian town of "Wo-ko-kon" (or Croatoan) would have been nearer the site of the wreck than "Se-co-ta." There may have been another town on the coast which has been omitted from the maps. The direction "southwest" would properly describe "Se-co-ta."

A group that calls itself "Croatan" still lives among the hills of North Carolina. They usually have English names. Archaeological surveys of the region by the National Park Service in 1938 located outlines of forts built by persons many assume were members of the Lost Colony.

The point I wish to make here is that very early in the history of the New World, white men (who were alone in a strange land, and because they were alone, were probably inclined to comingle with native Americans) were permanently ashore on the continent. Furthermore, this area was a part of the world where the Melungeons clearly could have originated.

**Roanoke Island**

The first settlement on Roanoke Island was in 1854. Officers of this settlement included the following men:

Philip Armadas
Arthur Barlow
John Wood
James Brownwich
Henry Greene
Benjamin Wood
Simon Ferdinando (believed to have been a Spanish spy)

Nicholas Petman
John Howes
William Greenville

Of all these names, note that only Ferdinando is non-English. According to Sams in the book mentioned above, this group took two Indians named Wan-chese and Manteo back to England. (It is believed that two Englishmen were left behind as hostages.) Manteo became a true friend of the English; he was born, and many of his kindred continued to live, in the coast town of Croatoan. (It appears to me that Croatoan—later Croatan—was the middle of three Indian towns situated toward the northern end of a sandy strip of land lying directly on the ocean between Hatteras and Ocracoke Inlets. It would lie somewhere on a straight line between those inlets and a point about eighteen miles southwest of Cape Hatteras, in what is now Hyde County, North Carolina.) I believe Manteo's connection to Croatoan and his friendship for the English may have been the trigger which later caused the members of the Lost Colony to turn to Croatoan as a haven of refuge. Other Indians of that village had also been particularly friendly, notably one "Tetepano," the husband of Manteo's sister.

By contrast, Chief Powhatan (of an area to the north, in the part of Virginia yet unexplored by the English) "viewed them with hostility, and although not once mentioned in these early narratives, he is yet said to have been responsible for their final destruction." (From the *Historic Travaile Into Virginia* by Stuckey, Library of Congress, pp. 85, 86, 89).

The second voyage to Roanoke Island (still according to Sams) was made by Sir Richard Grenville in 1685, from Plymouth, England. It had as principal "Gentlemen in the Company":

Raymond M. Stuckey
_____ Bremige
_____ Vincent
John Clark.

According to Sams, Grenville left fifteen Englishmen at Roanoke Island in 1585. They were later attacked by Indians from towns called "Se-co-ta a-quas-cog-c," and "Das-a-mon-que-pe-uc." Two were killed, and several others were wounded. *"They escaped to boats and fled toward Hat-o-rask, where they met four companions who had been hunting for oyster; all later departed, whither as yet, no one knows."*

Sams believes that "they attempted in their frail craft to coast down to Croatoan, where they knew they had friends, and perished by the way." All that was ever found of them were the bones of one on Roanoke Island, who had been slain by the "savages."

A fourth voyage, this one under the command of Captain John White, arrived at Roanoke Island in July of 1587. In this party were 150 men, including an old enemy, Simon Ferdinando, who had earlier abandoned the ship *Admiral* in the Bay of Portugal.

After Captain White and his crew arrived, they walked to the north end of the island, where a man named Ralph Lane, from an earlier voyage, had built a fort and a number of houses. The fort had been razed, and the houses were in a dilapidated condition. Captain White and his party despaired of ever finding any of the fifteen alive but did find the bones of one of them.

White gave orders to repair the houses and build more as needed. Then on the 28th of July, George Howe, one of Captain White's assistants, was slain by Indians as he waded, unarmed, in shallow water, catching crabs. White buried him, and two days later, on July 30th, passed by Croatoan Island with Manteo on the way to visit Manteo's kin and renew old friendships. On the 18th of August, Eleanor Dare, the wife of Annanias Dare and daughter of Governor White, bore a daughter they named "Virginia." She was the first English child born in the new world and was named for the settlement.

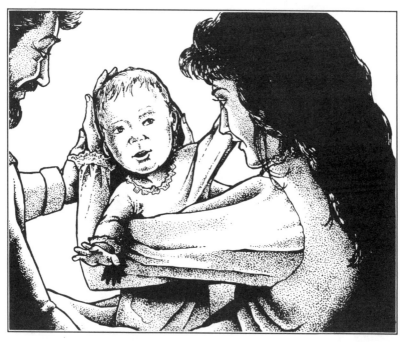

Soon afterward the little colony began to feel the need of supplies, but because of the existing war on the open seas with Spain, all were reluctant to make the voyage. Finally Governor White consented to go. The war, and especially the threatened invasion by the great Spanish armada, further delayed matters. The invasion seemed imminent, and an embargo was laid on all English shipping. Nevertheless, Sir Walter Raleigh succeeded in fitting out two ships for the colonists in Virginia, but they were attacked by Spanish cruisers and so badly damaged that they returned to England. Other attempts to send supplies to Virginia failed, and eventually all ships were diverted to oppose the great armada and save England. For that, the colony on Roanoke Island was lost forever.

The fifth and last voyage to Virginia was long delayed and was beset by numerous disappointments. Raleigh eventually obtained a license from the queen to send three ships in which a convenient number of passengers, pieces of furniture, and necessities were to be landed in Virginia. But the order was not obeyed. Rather, in contempt of the order by government officials opposed to it, White was denied the privilege of taking passengers or anything else in his original mandate; in the

end nothing went except the captains, the crews, and their chests.

Thus both masters and sailors were forced to disregard the interests of their countrymen in Virginia. For a time they did little more than remember Roanoke Island, concentrating instead on seizing Spanish ships and spoils, a task which consumed so many months that summer was almost gone before they reached the Virginia coast. That fall the weather was to be stormy and foul.

As night fell on August 12, 1588, they laid anchor at Hat-o-rask. They could see a great plume of smoke rising on Roanoke Island, near the place where they had left the colony. This smoke inspired them with hope that some might still be there.

On the 16th two boats went ashore and cannons were fired at intervals in an effort to locate the settlers, but to no avail. On the morning of the 17th, several men prepared to go up to the Roanoke settlement by water, but a gale broke on the bar, and a dangerous sea almost destroyed their boat. Seven of the crew drowned.

Finally, after much persuasion by Captain Cook and Governor White, they put off again from Hat-o-rask with nineteen men in two boats; it was dark when they landed, and they found they had missed their destination. They saw a great fire burning to the north and rowed toward it; as they neared the place, they sounded a trumpet, and afterward played many familiar English tunes, calling out in a friendly manner. There was no answer.

At daybreak they again landed, went to the fire, and found only burning grass and decayed trees.

From there they traveled through some woods but, finding nothing, went back to their boats and rowed to the place where White had left the colony months before. As they disembarked, they saw Indian footprints in the sand. On the bank they found a tree on which was carved the letters CRO; this, they believed, signified the place where they would find their lost comrades.

Next they saw an inland area enclosed by a tall palisade of tree trunks arranged to make a fortress. On the main post of the palisade, five feet off the ground, "in fair capital letters" was carved the word "CROATOAN." There was nothing else—no cross, no distress signal, nothing. Then the party saw where chests had been buried and dug up, goods spoiled by rain and tossed around, maps and books badly torn and damaged, armor corroded and rusty.

Severe storms struck the area and the party left. One ship's captain refused to do more and sailed for England; another postponed the return voyage "until a more convenient season" but did not go back to Roanoke Island. Eventually all three ships left, and the Lost Colony, if it was still alive, was gone forever.

According to the best information your author could find, 150 people had arrived when the settlement was made on January 7, 1587, and

more than two-thirds of them remained behind. While the actual number is a subject of disagreement, Sams says the following is an accurate listing of the men, women, and children "which safely arrived in Virginia, and remained to inhabit there." They number 115:

## Men

John White (Governor)
Roger Bailie (Assistant)
Annanias Dare (Assistant)
Christopher Cooper (Assistant)
Thomas Stevens (Assistant)
John Samson (Assistant)
Dyonis Harvie (Assistant)
Roger Pratt (Assistant)
George Howe (Assistant)
Simon Fernando (Assistant)
Nicholas Johnson (Assistant)

John Spendlove
John Hemmington
Edward Powell
Humfrey Newton
Thomas Gramme (probably the Scottish form of "Graham")
John Gibbes
Richard Shaberdge (Shabedge)
John Tydway
William Browne
Michael Myllet

Thomas Warner (Assistant)
Anthony Cage (Assistant)
Robert Wilkinson
Thomas Butler
Hugh Patterson
John Bridger
Grifen Jones (probably Welsh)
John Burden
John Cheven
Thomas Smith
William Willes
John Brooke
Cuthbert White
John Bright
Clement Tayler
William Sole
John Cotsmur
John Jones (possibly Welsh)
Ambrose Viccars
Edmund English
Thomas Topan
William Lucas
John Wright
William Dutton
John Chapman
Hugh Tayler
Michael Bishop
Richard Tompkins
Henry Mylton
William Nicholes
John Nichols
Morris Allen
William Clement
Richard Wildye (Wilde)

Richard Kemme
Richard Tauerner (Tavener)
Arnold Archard
John Wyles
George Martyn
Martyn Sutton
Mark Bennet
James Hynde
James Lasie (Lacy)
William Berde (Baird)
John Earnest
Thomas Harris
Thomas Hewit
Thomas Ellis
John Stilman
John Farre
Brian Wyles (possibly Willes)
Peter Little
Richard Berrye
Henry Berrye
Henry Johnson
John Starte
Richard Darige
William Waters
Robert Little
Lewes Wotton
Henry Rufoote
Charles Florrie
Thomas Harris
Thomas Scott
Henry Browne
Henry Payne (Paine)
John Borden

## Women

Elanyer Dare (wife of
   Annanias)

Agnes Wood (probably single)
Jane Jones

Elizabeth Glane (may be wife of Derby Glane, who deserted on Puerto Rico)
Alis Chapman (probably wife of John)
Elizabeth Viccars
Margery Harvie
Joyce Archard
Jane Pierce (probably single)
Audry Tappan (probably wife of Thomas Topan)
Margaret Lawrence (probably single)
Joan Warren (probably single)
Jane Mannering (probably single)
Rose Payne (probably single)
_____ Colman
Emme Merrimoth (probably single)

## Boys and Children

John Sampson
Thomas Archard
George Howe (probably son of George Howe, killed by Indians)
Robert Ellis
Thomas Smart
Ambrose Viccars
William Wythers
John Prat
Thomas Humfrey

## Children born in Virginia

Virginia Dare (daughter of Annanias and Eleanor)
_____ Harvie

## Fate of the Lost Colony

As I mentioned earlier, Croatoan (or Croatan) was an Indian village on one of the sandy strips lying between Pamlico Sound and the Atlantic Ocean. Apparently it was once called Abbot's Isle; in any case, it is the island now bounded by Hatteras Inlet on the north and Ocracoke Inlet on the south. It lies about fifty miles south of Roanoke Island.

Apparently the Lost Colony was massacred, *but some escaped.* Captain John Smith, in giving an account of a conversation he had with Powhatan during his captivity *(True Relations,* p. 28), says:

"What he knew of the Dominion he spared not to acquaint me with, as of certain men cloathed [like me] at a place called O-can-ho-nan."

Powhatan confessed that he had been at the murder of [white people] and, according to Smith

"showed a musket barrel and a brass mortar, and certain pieces of iron which had been theirs.

"We agreed with the King of Pas-pa-heigh [said Smith] to conduct two of our men to a place called Pan-a-wick [probably Pan-a-wa-i-oc, in Beaufort County, NC], beyond Roanoke [Island], where he reported many men to be appareled. We landed him at War-ras-koy-ack [an Indian town in what is now Isle of Wight County, VA] where, playing the villian and deluding us for rewards, he returned within three or four days later, without going any farther."

"Pas-pa-heigh" may be another name for Powhatan; in any event, he was not a friend like Manteo. (Smith also blamed the Indian priests that were connected with Powhatan for the slaughter of the white colony.) Regardless of who he was, some of the colonists almost certainly survived, for elsewhere we find:

"Where at Pec-car-e-cam-ek and O-chan-a-ho-en, by the relation of Ma-chumps [Powhatan's brother-in-law], people have houses with stone walls, one story above another, so taught them by the English who escaped the slaughter at Roanoke [Island], at what time this, our colony under the conduct of Captain Newport, landed within the Chesapeake Bay, where the people breed up tame turkeys about their houses, and take apes into the mountains [the English had never seen the mountains; "apes" may have been raccoons or opossums], and where, at Rit-a-noe, the Wer-o-once E-y-an-o-ce preserved seven of the English alive—four men, two boys, and one maid, who escaped and fled up the river of Chan-oke [Chowan] to beat his copper, of which he hath certain mines at said Rit-a-noe, as also at Pam-a-wank, are said to be a store of salt mines."

The clear implication is that some of the Lost Colony were killed, but others survived and probably lived out their days with the Indians. No record exists, of course, of their offspring.

## Some Final Traditions

In the Croatan tribe there is a tradition preserved of their historic friendship for the white man; it even says they took the English to live with them, where they (the English) became "incorporated" with the tribe. Soon after this incorporation, the tribe itself migrated westward to what is now Sampson County, North Carolina, and probably settled on the Lumber River in Robeson County as early as 1650. That is where they were found by the Huguenots in 1709, owning farms, having roads and other elements of civilized life. Their language was almost pure Anglo-Saxon, although they used many words which have long been obsolete in English-speaking countries (see the *Genesis of the United States*, Library of Congress, Volume 1, p. 185).

On a map made at the time to illustrate Captain John Smith's *True Relation*, there is a legend placed about the upper waters of the Neuse River:

"Here remaineth four men, cloathed, that came from Roanoke O-can-a-han-an [a town supposed to have been on the Neuse]."

Between the map's Roanoke and Tar (or Pamlico) rivers is another legend:

"Here the King of Pas-pa-hegh reported our men to be, and wants to go." [This seems to indicate a place in Dare, Tyrell, or Hyde County, the old Indian region of Se-co-tan. Near this legend is the word Pan-a-ni-eck.]

In the document *A True and Sincere Declaration* by the "Governors and Councillers of Virginia" written in 1609 (Library of Congress), the "Governors and Councillers" make this comment:

"[T]he intelligence of some of our nation planted by Sir Walter Raleigh [is] yet alive, within 50 miles of our fort (Jamestown), as testified by two of our colony sent out to seek them, who (though denied speech with them by the savage) found crosses and letters and characters and assured testamonies of Christians, newly cut in the bark of trees."

It seems certain, then, that at least a few of the Lost Colony survived, and I believe plausible conclusions as to what happened to them can be drawn from the evidence available. I think the English settlers had a plan to move and that the Indians knew of it. The reason they wanted to move was for protection from the storms that, even today, sweep in off the Atlantic and make life around Hatteras difficult at best. At first they wanted to go farther inland, but later decided to go to friendly Croatoan (even though it was a more exposed position) to wait for Governor White to return.

The Indians on the mainland were hostile, and all of them may have known of the colonists' planned move. Powhatan certainly knew, and probably concluded that their movement would mark a favorable time to strike. On Roanoke Island, the colonists were well protected by their fortifications, which had been built in Captain White's absence. And before White left, they had all agreed that if they found it necessary to go elsewhere, they would leave a sign, and carve a cross by it if they were in distress. No such cross was later found.

They were, in all likelihood, attacked as they made ready to leave by boat. The Indians could have been watching as they buried their chests and other articles too heavy to move to Croatoan. One of the settlers obviously stopped on the sandy bank of the island to leave an additional message for anyone reaching the island from England (the tree with the letters C-R-O); and it can be safely assumed that he was interrupted before he finished. At that point most of the colonists were probably slaughtered, *but a few may have escaped in boats up the Pamlico or the Neuse Rivers to O-can-ha-wan, or to Croatoan. All may have eventually joined the Croatoan tribe that later moved westward.*

The triumphant Indians probably swarmed into the fort, tore down the house, dug up the chests, destroyed or spoiled everything they did not want, and generally created havoc. No doubt they celebrated over the wretched prisoners, who were probably tortured to death; and any Indians who were their friends probably died with them.

Even though a few scattered survivors may have remained, the death blow to the colony had been struck, and the first attempt to settle "Virginia" had come to a bloody end.

## Other Legends

During the summer of 1939, Dr. H.J. Pearce, President of Breneau College, disclosed what he claimed to be a possible clue to the fate of the Lost Colony of Roanoke: a carved granite slab bearing ominous words. Dr. Pearce made no claim as to the authenticity of this slab. The Georgia educator had begun an intensive search into the fate of the Roanoke colonists in 1937, after an unidentified motorist supposedly stumbled upon a large piece of quartz some fifty miles inland from the site of the Lost Colony, on the bank of the Chowan River of North Carolina. Both stones, one of granite and the other of quartz, bore messages connecting them with the Lost Colony.

On one side of the quartz was this inscription:

"Annanias Dare & Virginia went hence to heaven 1591."

A plea for the transmission of "messages" to the Virginia Governor (John White) followed:

"Any Englishman shew John White Govr. Via."

And on the reverse side of the quartz was a seventeen-line message, which, translated freely from the Elizabethan, read:

"Father, soon after you went to England we came hither. Only misery and war for two years. Above half dead ere two years more from sickness, 24 surviving. A savage with message of a ship came to us. He repeated that after a small space of time the savages, afraid of revenge, had run away from island. We believe it was not you. Soon after this the savages, feigning the spirits were angry, suddenly murdered all save seven of us. My child, (Vir-gin-i-a), and Annanias too were slain with much misery. We buried all but four miles east of this river upon a small hill. Names all written there upon a rock. To any savage who will show this unto you, and show you hither, we promise to give plenty presents.

E.W.D."

The granite slab found two years later was about three and one-half feet long and fifteen inches wide, and a message carved upon it indicated that some of the colonists, after leaving their base on the North Carolina coast, moved southwest into South Carolina. Words carved upon it were in the same Elizabethan English as that found on the earlier piece of quartz, and may have been composed by Eleanor Dare, for the words "Father, we go SW" were carved along its edge. The rest of the message said:

"Here lieth Annanias Dare and Virginia. Father, savages murdered all save seven. Names written here. May God have mercy.

Eleanor Dare - 1591"

There followed the names of the victims:

"Sydor Boan Wilcan Birce Polle Carewe Bowman Spagne Tuckers Bolitoe Smythe Sakeres Holborn Winget Seate."

Not many of these names can be identified among the names of the

Roanoke island colonists, but it is entirely possible that some on either list were not interpreted correctly.

Dr. Pearce would not disclose the name of the person who found the granite stone. He had offered a 500 dollar reward for the piece after the earlier quartz message was found in North Carolina. Geologists who examined the carvings on both stones said it was possible that the messages had been written centuries before, and had survived the elements. Both stones, he said, were at Breneau College.

## The Lumber River

There is also a story I have heard of white people found on the Lumber River in Robeson County, North Carolina, by Huguenots in 1709. These people owned farms and spoke almost pure Anglo-Saxon. I will discuss them later in greater detail (see the "Lumbees" in Chapter Two).

## A Frenchman's Theory

According to Celestin Pierre Cambiaire, writing in *Officer d'Academie*

(The Mitre Press, London, 1935), inhabitants of what was then (as now) Hancock County, Tennessee, did not belong to "the same race" as the rest of the inhabitants of East Tennessee. He said:

"They have dark complexion, black hair, and brown eyes. Their type resembles the Indians. Their English is the English of two centuries ago. Their names are typically English. They claim Portuguese ancestry, but there is nothing in their names, language, or habits to justify that claim.

"The word Melungeon is evidently a slight transformation of the French word "Melangeon." The pronunciation of the "an" before a consonant, or at the end of a word in French, resembles that of "un" in English.

"The French came into Tennessee a long time before the English. In 1714 Charleville already had a store on the site where Nashville stands now. Some French traders or trappers must have given the name "Melangeons" to the descendants of a few white men and Indians who originated the strange race of people now lost among descendants of the first American pioneers.

"As 'Melangeons' (from the French word 'Melanger') means mixed breed, these people are that; but they have English names, and speak old-time English. They certainly have English ancestry.

"As their type [also] resembles the Indian type, it is clear that they have Indian blood. In the beginning of the English occupation of America, there was a considerable number of children born from English fathers and Indian mothers...

"Half-breeds were looked down upon, to a certain extent, by white people, and it is natural that some of them would have moved away to some remote place to form a new settlement. It seems that the Melungeons came into Hancock County between 1810 and 1851. [Hancock County was formed from Claiborne and Hawkins Counties in 1844; the Hawkins County Census of 1830 listed a large number of heads of households whose names were followed by f.c. (free persons of color).] They could not have invented this name [Melungeon], and they did not want it; and the few American settlers in Tennessee did not know enough French to originate it. Either the Melungeons brought the name with them after some Frenchmen gave it to them, or the name later followed them. They have no French ancestry, because if they did, they would not speak the English of about 200 years ago [400 years ago would have been more nearly correct, for Elizabethan English], and they would have at least a few French surnames.''

According to Mr. Cambiaire, practically all other East Tennessee inhabitants are descendants of English pioneers. He also said that this was true of Southwest Virginia (and was probably referring to Lee, Scott, Russell, and Washington Counties, all of which do have a percentage of Scotch-Irish and German settlers).

# Chapter Two
## OTHER POSSIBILITIES

### The Spanish

The people of Spain are a mixture of many different races: Iberians, Carthagenians, Phoenicians, Romans, Moors, and others. Spain's earliest inhabitants were Iberians. Their language and blood are preserved in the Basque Provinces in the northeastern part of the country; today, Basques claim to be the oldest race in Europe.

Then came Phoenician traders, who, passing the Pillars of Hercules at Gibraltar, founded Cadiz about 1100 B.C., as well as many other towns. Celtic tribes crossed the Pyrenees about 500 B.C. and mingled with the Iberians, begatting the Celtiberians.

Late in the third century B.C., Carthagenians made a settlement at Carthagena. Then came the Romans, who expelled the Carthagenians in 201 B.C., after the second Punic War. Spain became a Roman Province, and its inhabitants became Latins, contributing many famous names to Roman history and literature.

In the fifth century A.D., Vandals and Suevi overran Spain. On Rome's invitation, the Visagoths followed, overcame those invaders, adopted the Roman faith and tongue, and ruled the whole peninsula until the eighth century, when the Moslems began to make inroads. Roderick, the last of the Goths, fell in 711, in Andulusia, while fighting Berber hordes under Tarik. Then the Moors (or Saracens) mastered most of Spain, and during the eighth century they made an indelible impression on the Spanish race, language, customs, commerce, art, architecture, and culture. At the same time they themselves became Europeanized and were absorbed to a great extent.

The Goths, who originally came by invitation, were powerless to resist, as were the downtrodden Jews. On the whole, the native Spanish

placidly accepted conquest, until at last the Spanish "race" was little more than a mixture of distant peoples, with darker characteristics which, in many ways, were not unlike people of mixed race in America.

After all these wars, and after numerous constitutional struggles between monarchs, nobles, and the people, Ferdinand and Isabella came to the Spanish throne. Their marriage firmly united the Castille and Aragon Provinces in 1474. In 1492 they captured Granada, the Moors' last stronghold, then expelled both the Moors and the Jews. At about the same time, they inaugurated Spain's conquest of the New World, claiming (with Portugal) all the land in North America up to the 44th parallel. In the Mediterranean, Naples and Sicily were conquered in 1504; in the Americas, they advanced in Mexico, Peru, Chile, the West Indies, and Florida; and in Europe, France was humbled, and Francis I captured. Tunis in North Africa was taken in 1535, and Spain was a World Power to be reckoned with.

As you can see, through the Iberians, Carthagenians, Phoenicians, Celts, Vandals, Goths, Moors, and other peoples, it is conceivable that the Spanish Empire produced some ancestors of the Melungeons, as well as other "racial islands" in America. And even if they did not, it is instructive to study their history, for it is a broad print of the way different peoples mingle and affect each other in ways that are both mysterious and historical. On the following pages I will discuss the background and some of the characteristics of many of these groups, and you can form your own opinion as to their possible connection to the people who are the subject of this book.

## The Moors

### Of Antiquity

In the Middle Ages Morocco was a rich, powerful empire; trade with her was dangerous, but much sought after by Europeans. The present natives of Morocco are descendants of the fierce Berber tribe, who, along with the Arabs, overran Spain and established a Moorish kingdom.

During the eighteenth century the Salli Rovers, fierce Berber pirates, attacked the Mediterranean coast and sold thousands into slavery. They even invaded the British coast on occasion.

The Moors were given the name of ''Mauri'' by the Romans, who conquered many peoples of Northern Africa. The province established there by Rome was called Mauretania; the term is thought to have come from the Phoenicians, who arrived earlier. The inhabitants of Mauretania were Berbers, a white people whose ancestors were probably a mixture of the original Stone Age inhabitants of northwest Africa and earlier Mediterranean peoples who began moving west before 300 B.C. Both groups were white; both included members who were blond. The resulting Berber peoples were somewhat like Northern Europeans in build and complexion. The Phoenicians and Romans mixed little with the Berbers, except along the Mediterranean coast.

In the seventh century A.D., a band of aristocratic Arabs invaded northwest Africa. Having come without wives, they married Berber women, introduced Islam, and founded both dynasties and towns.

The first Moslem invasion of Spain came soon afterward. Most of the soldiers must have been Berbers; these were the people who set up the Moslem rule called the Caliphate of Cordoba; but the Caliphate fell, to be followed by a number of Arab kingdoms.

A second and more important migration of Arabs took place in the eleventh century; it was made up of two renegade Syrian tribes. An important mixture of Berbers, Arabs, and possibly blacks began at this time, for during this century blacks from the south of the African continent were brought as slaves to the northwest.

At the end of the eleventh century a fighting sect of Moors called Aloravides invaded Spain and swept away the Arab rulers. After fifty years they were, in turn, overthrown by another Moorish tribe, the Almorhades, who carried on a long and bitter fight against the Spanish. The Almorhades were defeated by the Spanish in 1212, and withdrew to Andalusia, where they founded the Kingdom of Granada. Their civilization at Granada rivaled the old Arab civilization of Cordoba; in fact, their art exceeded anything found in Christian Europe. The Moors have thus been credited with maintaining the spirit of civilization during the Dark Ages in Europe, creating, among other things, an original style of architecture. The Palace of Alahambra is still one of the world's most beautiful buildings.

In 1492, the year Christopher Columbus discovered America, Granada fell to Ferdinand and Isabella. Many Moors accepted the Christian religion, becoming known as Moriscas. They were the most peaceful and industrious inhabitants of Spain until the persecutions of Phillip II drove them to revolt.

The Moriscas were expelled from Spain in 1609; and while many of them returned to northern Africa, it is possible that some of them could have crossed the Atlantic, either as passengers, pirates, or explorers in their own right. They were unable to gain a foothold in Europe, although they did remain a menace to European trade and commerce. Some of them settled in coastal towns in North Africa and mixed with Arabs; others are said to have gone farther south, into the continent's interior. In general, persecutions in Spain up through 1809 were bad indeed: it is said that more than 31,900 people were burned alive. Especially hard hit were the Jews, the Moors, and the Moriscoes; Spain's population in those years decreased from ten to six million. Many left for distant parts of the world.

Up until the early part of the nineteenth century, the Moriscas were the dreaded pirates of the Mediterranean. Nations paid tribute for the privilege of letting their ships pass along the Barbary Coast. They often sold their captives as slaves or held them for ransom, and went unchecked until 1815, when they were beaten by the famous American Commodore, Stephen Decatur. Until that time, United States ships of commerce in the Mediterranean were also at their mercy.

For many years the Moorish or Barbary States of North Africa were controlled by Spain and France. The customs of the peoples of those states are Oriental; their speech is a form of Arabic, and they are Mohammedans.

## Of Today

Unlike their lowland cousins, today's mountain people of Morocco have lived in near isolation for centuries. Apparently their women do most of the work. Victor Englebert, writing in the June, 1968, issue of *National Geographic,* says that he once saw Moor women weave until 2:00 A.M., then nap until 4:00 A.M., rise, and grind barley on primitive hand mills for daily bread. The men, who are mostly shepherds, leave for the pastures about 8:00 A.M.; others who plow the fields, about an hour later. The plowmen are generally back home by noon, and for the rest of the day do only small jobs, such as crushing date pits for animal food.

These people are inhabitants of the Atlas Mountains, and are believed to be descendants of the original people of the Atlas. Some experts relate them to ancient Egyptians, but others say they come from southern Europeans of Iberian stock. They are, in any event, Morocco's first known inhabitants. They are fierce soldiers, as the French learned when they ruled a part of Morocco from 1912 through World War II. Subduing them was a bloody task that ended only in 1933.

As a group, the Moors have many characteristics that are common with the Melungeons; I have listed a few of them below.

(1) Many are mountain dwellers.

(2) Some of the Melungeons' physical features could be called Moorish.

(3) The fact that Moors generally were being persecuted on the Iberian Peninsula during the eighteenth century caused them to flee elsewhere.

(4) Both the Moors and the Melungeons were excellent drovers and herders of livestock.

(5) Many Melungeons have insisted that they are Portuguese (who also descended from invading tribes, including the Moors—see below).

## The Portuguese

The Portuguese lived on the southwestern coast of Europe, at the end of the Iberian Peninsula. From their earliest development they were sailors and seamen. Portuguese traders founded the first European colonies in many parts of the world.

The Golden Age of Portuguese history came in the late 1400s. During this time, Bartholmew Dias sailed around the Cape of Good Hope, and Vasco de Gama discovered a new route to India.

As with Spain, the people who first lived in Portugal were Iberians, but many other peoples invaded the country and mixed with the original settlers. These invaders included Phoenicians, Celts, Carthagenians, Romans, Greeks, Goths, and Moors. Even the Portuguese language is somewhat like Spanish, but softer and less emphatic. The Portuguese are both skilled fishermen and good farmers.

Phoenician and Carthagenian sailors came to Portugal in the 800s B.C. According to tradition, the Greeks founded colonies at the mouth of the Tagus River, where Lisbon now stands, in the 500s and 400s

B.C. The Romans settled in the region during their conquests in the 100s B.C. They called the area Lusitania, and it remained fairly stable for nearly 500 years. Then in 400 A.D. the Iberian Peninsula was invaded by the Visagoths, a warlike German tribe. They took it, and lived peacefully in both Portugal and Spain until the Moslem Moors conquered *them.*

Portugal prospered under its Moorish rulers, but by 1000 A.D. their power weakened, and the Spanish Christians began to conquer the whole of the Iberian Pennisula. In the early 1580s King Phillip II of Spain seized the Portuguese throne, and Spain held it until 1685.

Portugal began its overseas expansion in 1415, establishing colonies in India in the 1500s (Goa, Damas, and Diu), and in other parts of the world. It is not beyond the realm of possibility that some Portuguese sailors could in fact be ancestors of the Melungeons, for their unrecorded explorations could easily have reached into North America.

## The Berbers, Shaw-Berbers, the Tuaregs and the Rifs

The Berbers live along the western part of Mediterranean Coast of Africa, and in the Sahara Desert. They are much like the Arabs in customs and religion (which is Moslem). They speak the Hametic and Arabic languages. They vary in appearance from light hair and fair skin (like the Rifs in Morocco) to dark skin and curly hair (like the Kobyls in Algeria).

The Shaw-Berbers live on farms in the Atlas Mountains. The Tuaregs roam the deserts looking for grass for their animals. Rifs (or Riffians) are Hamites of the Moslem faith who have frequently revolted against the government of Morocco. All of these peoples are somewhat like our Melungeons in both physical characterics and habits, so they, like the Guineas (below) are included here as possible Melungeon ancestors.

## The Guineas

Guinea is a district of West Africa stretching along the shore of the Gulf of Guinea between Senegal and Cape Negro. It is divided into Upper and Lower Guinea, and includes French, Spanish, and Portuguese Guinea, as well as the Guinea Islands. Little is known of the natives.

Mr. W.H. Gilbert of the Library of Congress has done extensive research on a group of people in the mountainous area of West Virginia.

This group is very similar to the Melungeons, but are known as "Guineas." Could they possibly have originated in one of the West African Guineas? Nothing can be said with certainty. To compound the puzzle, Mr. Gilbert has said that these people bear resemblence in both features and customs to a "racial island" of people in the neighboring state of Maryland. The latter group, however, are often called "Wesorts," a word thought to be coined from their own expression "We sorts are not like you sorts."

## The Phoenicians

The Phoenicians lived in the coastal region of Syria. Their country was under the overlordship of Egypt from about the sixteenth century B.C. on and suffered from the invasions of the Hittites from Asia Minor in the centuries that followed.

After Egyptian rule began to decline in the late fourteenth century B.C., theirs became a flourishing and independent country; its most important cities were Tyre and Sidon. The Phoenicians began to colonize the islands of the Mediterranean as well as the coast of North Africa, including Carthage, Hippo, Utica, and Tripoli. They were a trading race and were reputed to have had dealings with Solomon. They also visited Britain in search of tin.

In the ninth century B.C., their country was invaded by the Assyrians, and became a dependency of the Assyrians until the late seventh century B.C. After numerous revolts, Phoenicia became virtually independent. Then, about 605 B.C., it was subdued by Nebuchadnezzer, and became a part of the Babylonian Empire.

Following the Persian Conquest in 537 B.C., Phoenicia became a part of the Persian Empire, and remained so until the coming of Alexander the Great in 333 B.C. Then Phoenician trading began to decline, and a part of Phoenicia passed to Egypt. Most of it eventually came into the possession of the Ptoemies, and remained so until the first century B.C., when it fell under the dominion of Tigranes of Armenia. It was conquered by Pompeii in 64 B.C., and thus became part of the Roman Province of Syria.

The Phoenicians were traders between the East and the West, and because of that their race spread far beyond their borders. Among their important industries were dyeing with Tyrian purple, linen-weaving, glass-making, and metal working. Aegean civilization is supposed to have been derived from the contact with the Phoenicians who, in passing knowledge from Egypt and Babylonia, are also credited with the early use of an alphabet, forming an important link in the chain of civilization. Their contribution to the characteristics of any of the races of the Western Hemisphere can only be speculated upon, but in some of their physical characteristics they are not unlike the people who are the subject of this book.

## The Celts

Among the early invaders of Portugal were the Celts, who were also among the earliest groups of "Aryan" inhabitants of Southwest Europe. There were two main branches of the Celts:

(1) The Cadhelic, comprising the highlanders of Scotland, Ireland, and Manx, and the Cymric branch that included the Welsh and Bretons.
(2) The Celtriberians (compounded from Celt and Iberian), who were supposedly the original inhabitants of Spain. This could provide a partial explanation for the Welsh as a possible origin of the Melungeons.

## The Gypsies (Romanies, Romanos)

"Gypsy" is a name given to a nomadic race found in Europe, Asia, and America. In England they have been called Egyptians, Greeks, "heathens," and Bohemians. They call themselves Romanies or Romanos. Their language, which is the same in all countries, is Romani Chiv. They are described by themselves as "little Egyptians."

Gypsies probably appeared in Europe during the early part of the fourteenth century, and reached England at its close. At first they were well-received in Europe, for many were skilled metal workers, but later charges of kidnapping and other crimes were brought against them. Some were mercilessly hunted down and put to death.

Gypsies of past centuries have been famous for their skill in music and dancing, and in later years for horse-trading and fortune-telling. They conform to no religion, and their moral codes are far from strict. Their physical characteristics are: lithe figure, olive skin, dark lustrous eyes, exceedingly fine teeth, and black (or dark) hair.

## The Arabs

"Arab" is the general word for the peoples who inhabit Arabia, parts of North Africa, Mesopotamia, the coast of the Red Sea, and the Persian Gulf; and for those who conquered Spain and other parts of Southern Europe during the Middle Ages.

The purest type is found in the neighborhood of Hadramet and Yemen, and among the Bedouin nomads of the Central Arabian deserts. Arabs along the coast are often of very mixed descent. The so-called "pure-blooded" Arabs are tall, lean, long-limbed, and muscular. They are brown-skinned, black-eyed, and oval-faced, with handsome features and beautiful teeth. While at times capable of treachery, they are a proud race, and are hospitable to strangers.

## The Syrians

Syria belonged to the Egyptians and partly to the Hittites about the middle of the second millenium, B.C. The Phoenicians became powerful a few centuries later, and founded a kingdom, which came (successively) under the domination of Assyria, Babylonia, Persia, Macadon, the Seleucids, Rome, Byzantium, and the Arabs. It was taken by the Turks in 1516. Napoleon's invasion in 1799 was followed by an Egyptian occupation in 1831 through 1841.

Their Aramaic dialect is more elastic than Hebrew, probably due to the Greek tongue from which Syria borrowed much of its vocabulary.

## The Greeks

The present Greek populations include three main stocks:

(1) Aboriginal Mediterranean brunettes, the purest found in Crete.
(2) Dark, sallow brachycephalic Alpine highlanders, typically represented in Albania.
(3) Scanty remains of tall, fair, or ruddy persons, whose successive invasions marked the turning point of Aegean history, as follows:
    (a) Thraco-Phrygian, about 1500 B.C.
    (b) Galatian, 275 B.C.
    (c) Dorian, 100 B.C.; and others

It is mainly the Albanian blood which differentiates modern from ancient Greeks.

## The Romans

Who can contest the Roman contribution to world history? Who knows the true reach of their sprawling empire? The traditional date of the founding of Rome is 753 B.C., by Romulus. He allowed the Sabines to settle on Capitoline Hill and amalgamate with the Romans. He also divided citizens into three tribes: Ramnes, Tities, and Luceres.

Tullus Hostilius (673-642 B.C.), after destroying Alba Longa, allowed the inhabitants to settle on the Caelian Hill and become the first members of the Plebian Order.

The Etruscan Lucias Tarquinias Priscus (616-578 B.C.) probably represents a foreign dynasty thrust upon the Romans after subjugation by their Etruscan neighbors, and whose rule was probably thrown off in 509 B.C., after which they seized the Roman territory on the right bank of the Tiber. There was a war with the Latins until 493 B.C., and the joint attack of the Latins and the Greeks on the Etruscans brought about their final decline, Etruria having been planted with Roman colonies.

The great Gallic invasion and sacking of Rome in 390 B.C. followed. The three Punic Wars in 264-241 B.C., 218-201 B.C., and 149-146 B.C. resulted in the formation of the Roman Provinces of Sicily, Corsica, Hither and Further Spain, and Africa.

Gaul was subjugated in 181 A.D. Britain was lost to the empire in 407 A.D., and Rome itself was sacked in 410 A.D. by Alaric, the Visagoth. Goths and Franks settled in Gaul, and the Vandals settled in Spain (433-455 A.D.). In 455 A.D. Rome was sacked again, this time by the Vandal Genseric, and the Visagoths took posession of what remained of the Western Roman Empire.

## Native Americans

### The Cherokee

Since the Cherokee Indians lived the southeastern United States, in the general area where the earliest Melungeons were found, they cannot be ruled out as possible ancestors of the Melungeons, yet there is no strong supporting evidence for this possibility. The Cherokee did live in the southern Appalachians during the 1700s, and fought the white colonists in the Carolinas; they even sided with the British during the American Revolution. However, their connection to the origins of the Melungeons remains speculative at best.

### The Yuchi (Children of the Sun)

The Yuchi are designated members of the Creek Confederacy by ethnologists, historians, and the United States Indian Office, although some members of the tribe insist that they be treated as a separate nation. Dr. John R. Swanton, a recognized authority on the Creek Indians, has said that the earliest mention of the Yuchi (also called the Chisca) is found in early Spanish documents, "published and unpublished." The connection of the Yuchi to the Melungeons is not much stronger than the Cherokee connection, but they have been known to have Melungeon mates.

The Yuchi believe that they derive their origin from the sun. More than one band are known to have lived in the southeastern United States. They are one of the few small groups in eastern North America having an independent stock language. Legends among them have led them to believe that they are the most ancient inhabitants of this part of the continent, but that is not certain.

The Yuchi were visited by De Soto and other early explorers. De Soto sent soldiers to the Chisca Province, which was evidently located in the rougher parts of what is now Tennessee. According to Dr. Swanton, some of the Yuchi left the Appalachian Highlands because of the colonial wars, and in 1656 a part of the tribe settled on the James River in Virginia. They defeated the colonists in battles, but were not heard of afterwards.

It appears that they separated into distinct groups. One remained in the north (Tennessee); a second group settled not far from the Choctawhatchee River in western Florida; and others established themselves on or near the Savannah River in Georgia. Dr. Swanton points out a reference to the "Uche" or "Round Town People" in South Carolina state archives. He also mentions a legend found by Thomas Jeffery at some point on the Savannah River above Augusta, which read:

"Hughchees or Hogoloes Old Town deserted in 1715."

"Hughchees" supposedly means "Yuchis."

In about 1729, the Yuchi gathered in a settlement on the Chattahoochee River under the protection of the Creek Confederacy. In about 1791, William Bartram, a botanist, visited that area in search of botanical specimens. He described the town as the largest, most compact and best situated Indian town he had ever seen.

"The houses had wooden frames, lathed and plastered inside and out with a reddish, well-tempered clay, or mortar, that looked like red brick walls. They were neatly covered with cypress bark and shingles."

Whether this means they had earlier been influenced by the habits of European explorers is a matter for speculation. A United States Commissioner to the Creeks saw something similar in 1785 and said:

"These people are more civilized and orderly than their neighbors. Their women are more chaste, and the men are better hunters.

"They have lately begun to settle out in the villages, and are industrious compared with their neighbors. The men help the women at their labors and are more constant in their attachment to the women than is usual."

Timothy Barnard, a British subject and "man of affairs," married a Yuchi and acquired great influence in Indian affairs. He was the first white settler in Macon, Georgia, and died in 1820. He had three sons by his Yuchi wife: Timpoochee, Michee, and Cosena. These children later played important roles in the government of the Creek Nation, after its removal to the "Indian Territory."

A great grandson of Cosena Barnard was the Reverend Noah G. Gregory, who served as a representative from his native town to the Creek Nation, Indian Territory. That the "Euchees" were essentially a distinct tribe from any others is indicated by their language (which has no resemblance to any tongue spoken on the continent) and by their customs and personal appearance. They differed from other aboriginal tribes, for many of them had gray eyes and their complexion was several shades lighter than the full-blooded members of other nations. The shape of their faces seemed to differ slightly, too, and the women, in many instances, were exceedingly beautiful.

Yuchis, like the Croatoans, were friendly to the white man. They even allied themselves with the United States in 1814, against the Creeks. They were led by Timpoochee Barnard, the son of the British subject (actually, a Scotchman). Timpoochee also served in the Confederacy during the Civil War.

Yuchis were very superstitious. As late as 1890, most of them believed implicitly in witchcraft. They were once noted for pottery made by the women  and for clay pipes made by the men. Dr. Swanton believed they had a distinct culture that complemented their distinct language.

Some believe the Yuchi to be survivors of the friendly native Americans who greeted Columbus when he first landed in the New World. They also believe Yuchis could have descended from the Lucayans, Indians thought to have fled to Andros Island a hundred miles off the Florida coast to escape the "fire stick" of Columbus. In an ancient Spanish chronicle, the Lucayans of the Bahamas were called "Yucayas," and the Indian name for the "Columbus Indians" was "Yuchi."

Their later history, like that of the Melungeons, is easier to reconstruct in later years. A prominent member of the Yuchi in the Creek nation after their removal to the "Indian Territory" was Chief Samuel William Brown (1843-1935). His son, Chief Samuel William Brown, Jr. (1879-1957), visited the state of Georgia a short time before his death. From his father's vivid descriptions, he was able to recognize various places. He declared that the Yuchi had inhabited Georgia for a thousand years, and spoke of their having lived in an area of the coast now submerged. Brown also knew of a tradition that said the Indians had come from the famous Easter Island.

Several Yuchi returned to visit Phoenix City, Georgia, in June of 1958, when a hundred acres of land were dedicated for restoring the Yuchi town in the Columbus-Phoenix area. This land was presented to Georgia under the auspices of the Columbus Museum of Arts and Crafts.

## The "Lumbees"

In an earlier chapter I mentioned the legend of the white people found on the Lumber River in Robeson County, North Carolina. They were found by the Huguenots in 1708, and were said to have owned farms and lived in a "civilized manner" (meaning, presumably, like Europeans). They are also reputed to have spoken an older form of English.

In the October 30, 1966, issue of the *Baltimore Sun,* a writer named Mary Conelly published an interesting feature article on the "Lumbees." She appears to follow with some degree of accuracy the dates and events given in printed accounts of the "Lost Colony" of Roanoke Island. At that time (1966) the Lumbees had been migrating to Baltimore for the preceding 24 years, partly because of the effects of automation on North Carolina's farms. Baltimore for them became the most convenient industrial center where jobs could be had.

Once there they became more of a colony than a tribe. They managed to locate close together in east Baltimore, where their number eventually ran into the thousands. Other Lumbee families were scattered throughout metropolitan Baltimore. Their population in Robeson County had dwindled for years, as they had left in families and in groups. Miss Conelly says that "whatever happened to the Lumbees before [their settlement in North Carolina] is an open question but [it is certain] that the white man had some part in it." Their complexions vary from dark to very fair; it is not unusual to see blue eyes and blond hair among them. She says that even though Lumbees who are strangers can recognize each other, their features, unlike those of the Cherokees, do not conform to any particular pattern.

No trace remains of their original language, and Miss Conelly says that it is as if they have always spoken English. Their first names, for example, are names like these: Chavis, Berry, Hunt, Lowry, Costmore, Locklear, Oxendine, and Sampson. One of them told her that there were no "Running Deer" or "Hungry Bear" among them.

Even the Lumbees themselves are unsure of their heritage. They say they have been called "Croatans," "Cherokee," and just plain "Indians of Robeson County." The name "Lumbee" is apparently derived from the Lumber River, or the town of Lumberton, North Carolina. Some of the Lumbees prefer to be classified as descendants of the Lost Colony, while many Robeson County Indians continue to call themselves "Cherokee." Cherokees in western North Carolina, however, deny kinship to them.

For some reason the Indians of Robeson County do not like to be called Croatans. Miss Conelly discusses the English voyages to settlements at Roanoke Island between 1580s and '90s, when Governor White went back to England for supplies and finally returned to find the place abandoned, overrun, and in a state of ruin. Miss Conelly says that if the Lumbees are descended from the Lost Colony their ancestral tribe was the Hatteras, and that it was the Hatteras of the "Algonquian linguistic stock" with whom the Sixteenth Century English had their first contact. The Lumbees may be right.

She also mentions the fact that two members of the tribe were taken to England, along with a cargo of tobacco and potatoes (later called "Irish potatoes"). These two were Manteo and Wanchese, of course. She quotes Mr. George Percy of the original Jamestown colony, who wrote of seeing in the Virginia-North Carolina area

"a savage boy about the age of ten years, which had a head of perfect yellow hair and a reasonable white skinne, which is a miracle amongst the savages."

Other early Virginia historians quoted by Miss Conelly include John Lawson, who, shortly after 1700, wrote this about the Hatteras:

"They tell us that several of their ancestors were white people, and could talk in a book, as we do, the truth of which is Confirmed by gray eyes being found frequently amongst *these* Indians, and no others...

The Hatteras provided the English with rather more than relief and conservation. During a several-years' war with the Tuscarora Indians, which began in 1611, the Hatteras fought loyally on the colonists' side."

Other tribes listed by Miss Conelly as living in the area were Chowanocs, Catawbas, Cherokees, and these Siouan tribes: Waccamaw, Peedee, Winyaw, Cape Fear, and Cheraw.

Miss Conelly's illustrations show the Lumbees to have dark complexion and dark hair, in many cases; and that some are rather beautiful, and obviously talented. She says:

"If they are not 'Croatoans,' and yet are descendants of English settlers who spoke Elizabethan English, then they could have descended only from the 1685 colony of Sir Richard Grenville, fifteen of whom were left behind. Two were killed, and others wounded. They escaped in boats and fled toward Haterask, where they met four companions, hunting oysters, and departed, whither as yet no one knows."

She then gives the following summary:

"Historians agree that it was the Hatteras with whom the English colonists had their first contacts, but they do not agree that the Lumbees are necessarily of Hatteras descent."

Opposing views seem to be that the Lumbees are descended from the Cheraws, a Siouan tribe, first encountered in South Carolina by De Soto in 1540. After that date, this tribe is thought to have made its way westward to Robeson County.

# Chapter Three
## OTHER SIMILAR GROUPS

In 1926 Arthur H. Estabrook of the Carnegie Institution and Ivan E. McDougle of Goucher College co-authored a book called *Mongrel Virginians.* Included was a contribution from the Department of Genetics of the Carnegie Institution. This book, published by the Williams and Williams Company of Baltimore, contains much that merits repeating here. The authors were careful to conceal the names, nicknames, and locations of their subjects by giving them such names as the "Win" tribe of "Ab" County, the common surnames "Jones," "Brown," etc. Their real names were something entirely different.

The first group covered in this research was a group in a county in Virginia. This state has had a vital statistics law since 1853, and with the exception of the years 1896 and 1912, it has been possible to check the Federal Census records decade by decade and complete a family tree on this group to the present generation.

The two authors, one a specialist in eugenic research and the other in social research, have explored the historic and genetic background of the small, so-called red-black-white groups who have lived in the same localities for over a hundred years.

The anonymous "Ab" County lies in the foothills of the Blue Ridge, and its mixed-blood group, the "Win" tribe, is the subject of most of the rest of this chapter. This tribe was found to be neither black nor white, but by its own claim Indian; in reality it is probably a mixture of all three races. The Wins lived in an area eight miles long and one to four miles wide and numbered about 500 people, residing generally in log houses or rough shacks. They were usually renters, although some owned both houses and land. Their main source of income came from tobacco farming and sharecropping; a few worked as laborers for nearby farmers.

One church mission school offered them all the formal education they received. They also maintained a chapel, although transportation over dirt roads was difficult in the winter months. The Wins took no part in activities outside their own area; the whites ignored them, the blacks resented them, and the natural result seemed withdrawal. They were generally referred to as "yellow negros," Indians, or "mixed"; no one called them whites. They themselves generally claimed Indian descent, although they were conscious of a mixture, and preferred the term "Indian" when they had to choose. A few claimed to be white.

A term used to designate black slaves who had been given freedom by their owners before the Civil War was "free persons of color." Such persons were thought to have mated with each other or with the mixed-race Indians around the county. (The "free" blacks were looked down upon by other blacks and were unable to associate with the whites since the social structure established by slavery was ruptured. This pattern was slow to change after the civil war and was not a subject of study by the authors of the book.)

During the early 1920s, sociology students in Virginia assisted in gathering data on the Win group, which had never been studied seriously. Only one article on the Wins had appeared in the *Richmond Times-Dispatch* prior to 1920 although some religious missionary publications did carry a few short articles about them in the years after the Win mission was founded (about 1900). The study by the students, completed in 1923, also used fictitious names and showed that the Wins started from four sources. These sources were called "fountainheads." One was a white man they named "Brown," and the other three were Indians they called "Lane," "Thomas," and "Jones." Black blood present in the group, they said, appeared later.

Briefly, a white man named Brown married "Dolly Thomas," either a full-blood or a half-blood Indian. They had many children by the name of Brown, and those children, in turn, married. Their descendants were (in 1923) found in the "Coon Mountain" region of Ab County.

Dolly Thomas's father, William Thomas, was known to have been an Indian and to have lived on the "Ban" River in that county. No one knew, however, from what tribe he came; it could have been Cherokee from the southern Appalachians, Powhatan from eastern Virginia, or Tuscarora from southeastern Virginia. It is evident, however, that they were wandering Indians since Ab County never belonged to any particular tribe. Legend said that William's ancestors were traveling from the Carolinas to Washington to see the "Great Father" just after the Revolution, and a few stopped off in Ab County.

Another daughter of William Thomas married Ed Jones, an Indian, in 1790; the official record of the marriage was found in the Ab County Courthouse. The license does not give the race of the two parties; these were deduced from statements made by Ab County people and some of the older Wins.

A son of Ed Jones, Ned, was born about 1791; he was, of course, of mixed blood and married his first cousin on his mother's side, a girl named Iders. The Joneses multiplied, and by 1925 they made up at least half of the Win population of the area.

A third Indian strain in the Wins came through "John Lane," a full-blooded Indian born in 1780. His daughter married into the mixed-blood Brown family, and with the others mentioned above, settled down on or near Coon Mountain, about seven miles west of the Ab County Courthouse.

Their children intermarried with each other and with a few white families nearby. Matings of an illegitimate nature apparently took place with blacks as well—some slave, some free, the latter being referred to as "the free issue."

These early mixtures caused a social separation from the whites of the area. Apparently the blacks also disdained the mixture, especially during the period before the Civil War, when slavery still existed. This brought on a further social segregation until, after a time, the "Browns" and the "Joneses" became a separate group, the "Wins."

In a pamphlet called "Surviving Indian Groups," Mr. W.H. Gilbert of the Government and General Research Division, Library of Congress, refers to the Piedmont and Blue Ridge Indian-mixed-bloods as follows:

"Beginning with Rappahannock County in the north, and continuing southward along the Blue Ridge, through Rickbridge and Amherst Counties, and striking directly southward to Halifax County, on the North Carolina border, we find small colonies of mixed people who claim Indian descent, and are most generally called 'issues.'

"Amherst County 'issues': This group of about 500 or 600 mixed-bloods is located in the central part of Amherst County, about four or five miles west of the county seat. The principal settlements are on Bear Mountain and Tobacco Row Mountain, in the Blue Ridge.

"At the extreme western end of the county is another mixed group of similar origin, derived from Indian, white, and in some localities, black blood. An Episcopal mission for the 'issues' is located three miles west of Sweet Briar College and comprises a school and other facilities.

"The typical 'issue' is a very rich brunette with straight black hair and caucasian features. The chief family names are: Adcox, Branham, Johns, Redcross, and Willis.

"In the bottoms the 'issues' raise tobacco, while on the slopes corn and oats are grown. They are mostly renters and truck farmers. The white neighbors of these people are said to regard them as mulattoes. (The term 'issue' is applied to mixed bloods of the same type in many of the counties of Virginia.)

"To the northwest of Amherst County, in Rockbridge County, is a small group located on Irish Creek, not more than twelve miles east of Lexington, Virginia, and called 'Brown People.' Their number is estimated at over 300, and they show a mixture of white, Indian, and occasionally black blood. Like the 'issues' of Amherst County, they are a group apart from both whites and blacks....

"The remnants of Indian blood in Virginia can be divided into the Tidewater group and the Piedmont-Blue Ridge group. Both have lost their Indian language and traditions almost entirely, but the Tidewater group still maintains a tribal organization and, in some instances, territorial reservations. The upland group shows no tribal organization but tends to retain traditions of Indian origin."

These seven paragraphs serve to explain and identify the anonymous Virginia groups given by Estabrook and McDougle. I will continue below with further descriptions of these Piedmont-Blue Ridge groups, as given by the authors of *Mongrel Virginians:*

**The White-Brown Family**

According to land records at Richmond and in Ab County, the Brown family was migrating west along the James River about 1730, and it is assumed that these Browns are white, of English descent. In 1769, a Robert Brown was living on his own land of several hundred acres on the south side of "Jones" Creek in Ab County. He died in 1778, leaving some property to his three sons. The inventory of his estate shows a personal property value of twenty-five thousand dollars, which included a number of slaves, one of whom was valued at eight hundred dollars.

When Robert's son Bill died, Bill's personal estate was twenty-five hundred dollars, a "goodly amount" in the latter part of the eighteenth century. One son, Andy Brown, also lived in Ab County; he married in 1794 and died in 1801, leaving five children. Three of these were married in Ab County after 1822. Later the entire family went west, and the only trace of them ever found was in a county in Illinois in 1848, where a son was recognized as "a prominent citizen and grocer."

Another son of Bill Brown was the William Brown we have mentioned earlier. As you will recall, he married Dolly Thomas, and their numerous descendants remained in Ab County in the Coon Mountain area. The fate of Bill's third son is not given.

There was a legend that the Browns were Portuguese, but the researchers failed to uncover any factual supporting information.

## The Indian Browns

The Browns were the aristocrats of the Wins. This family had less mixing with blacks, and felt itself superior to the Joneses, who apparently had more of such mixing. (Some of the Blacks, a branch of the Joneses, had "decidedly" black features.) In any case, Bill Brown built a house in a little cove on the east side of the mountain, where he lived a retiring life, dying in 1861. Nothing is known of his wife other than her stock, Indian, and that she was dark. Their six children were also dark-skinned, with long black hair and typically Indian makeup. They were not white, but neither did they consider themselves black. They were reported in early census records as the usual "free persons of color."

The fate of the eldest of their six children is not known, although he was the father of an illegitimate child by a white woman in 1848. She later married another one of the Joneses.

Their second child, also a son, was typically Indian, with copper-colored skin. He had no education but did eventually acquire some land through his father because he once sold 150 acres on Coon Mountain for one dollar per acre. His second wife, one Susie Johnson, was white, and they had fourteen children. Some were darker than others, but all were characteristically Indian.

The fate of Bill Brown's other four children is not noted. However, a study of some of the fourteen grandchildren sired by Bill's second son gives an interesting insight into the evolution of the Indian Browns.

The oldest of the grandchildren was Amelia Brown. When she was young she was "called very good looking." At age 18 she had an illegitimate child, Amanda, by a white man from another state. Then she bore another, named Eloise, who, in 1867, married a cousin, Adam Brown. Adam looked like an Indian but had "long, tight corkscrew curls" and was medium dark. Apparently he was not very alert mentally and became an uneducated laborer as did other Wins of this period.

Amelia had four children by Adam. Alice, born in 1871, had copper-colored skin and curly black hair. She learned to read and write but "was not very intelligent, was unchaste, and would steal." She married a Jones cousin, had several children, and apparently maintained a very low standard of living in her home.

Amelia's fourth child, Alexander (also called Alec) was born in 1872. He left the Win region but was said to have stayed in the same county and lived with his father's last wife. He was a "typical Win," unintelligent and "very stubborn in makeup." He was a farm hand and never married.

Amelia separated from Adam in 1873. She later had two more illegitimate children: the first, Alfred, became a laborer, and was reportedly "a good hand to work, but unambitious, inefficient, dishonest, and weak in character." One person the researchers interviewed called him "the meanest scoundrel in the county." He married a woman named Louise Hall in 1905, and they had eleven children. They separated because of her "licentious behavior" in taking up with Adelbert Brown, another Win.

Louise Hall was the daughter of Andrew Hall, a light mulatto, and Lu Ethel Black, a Jones. She had no Indian characteristics, and apparently gave the impression of being a "mean white woman with a little black in her." Intellectually, she was "of fair ability, more capable than her husband."

All of Alfred and Louise's children had "fair ability" in school. Their eldest daughter reached the 7th grade and later worked as a house maid, doing well until March of 1924, when she had an illegitimate child. The father was given as "being in question...."

Alva Brown, Amelia's last illegitimate child, was sired by a white. Alva had no "schooling" and became a tenant farmer. In 1902 he married Athena Brown, daughter of Abigail Brown, and together they had six children. Some years later he moved from the Win area to the western part of Virginia.

Athena Brown was practically white, and she died of pneumonia during the great flu epidemic of 1918. One of her sons moved to Georgia, and two moved to Lynchburg, Virginia. The others went with their father. Nothing is known of the traits of the children except that "one daughter was a prostitute." After Athena's death, Alva reportedly lived with a black woman.

Amelia died in 1903. One of her brothers was Alphonse, a typical Indian who worked hard and acquired a little land. Although he was not educated, he was a man of good character. He married a woman named Belle Jones, an industrious soul also of good character but reputedly of such low intelligence she could barely read or write. They had ten children, all of whom I shall describe briefly:

First son: Copper colored skin, uneducated, a farm laborer, cohabited with an illegitimate Brown. He was white in complexion but mentally defective; he was always disagreeable and suspicious.

Second son: Had "huge, coarse features, yellow copper-tinted skin; was an alcoholic and a browbeater; sometimes threatened to 'shoot and kill.' Served time for various misdemeanors."

Third son: Was yellow-haired and copper-skinned; never attended school; remained on the same rented farm for years; married a Jones (who attended school from age 7 to 14 but never progressed beyond the third grade); had a "meek disposition" and was a hard worker. They named their oldest child for a patent medicine [not given], and could not spell his name without referring to the label on the bottle.

Fourth and fifth sons: Twins. One married an illegitimate Jones girl, was practically white, and lived as a tenant farmer. The other twin had straight black hair, copper-colored skin, and "there was nothing against him."

Sixth son: Did not enter school until fourteen; was a very slow learner;

became a tenant and supported his mother. He was also secretary and treasurer of the mission chapel.

Seventh child, a daughter: "Did not have good sense." In school she was continually fighting with other children. She had deformed feet, and needed institutional care.

Eighth child, a son: Honest and truthful, a hard worker but slow in school.

Ninth child, a son: Almost as defective mentally as his sister.

Tenth child: Gender unknown; may have died young.

The Indian Browns continued in much the same way on through the next generation, when the research ended.

## The Indian Joneses

We mentioned earlier that a daughter of William Thomas married an Indian named Ed Jones in 1790. The common mother of the Joneses was a sister of the common mother of the Browns, so that many of the same biological characteristics (probably Indian) were found in both families. The name (Jones) was a white name, and was found in "Ac" County, Virginia, at about the same time it appeared in "Ab" county. Ed came out of the mountains, was partly white, but had "black hair and complexion, but without a nappy head." Evidently he was also part Indian.

Ed's son, Ned, married a girl named Iders (probably her given name), and their first son, Hal, was born about 1810. Hal married a girl named Ada in 1830; Ada was also part Indian, and they had a number of children.

Their oldest son was referred to as "seven-eighths black," by one person interviewed, but with straight hair. Another described him as a "dark blue Indian." He became a carpenter, good in woodcraft and basketry, but without a formal education. He owned land that was given to him by his father. He was also described as lazy and a hypochondriac. He married a woman named Hill, but they soon separated; then he lived with a Brown. There is no record of his having married her, but they had fourteen children.

Hal's second son never went to school and was mentally slow. Apparently he rented part of a farm for over twenty years and built a good reputation. He also maintained a fair standard of living, marrying a woman named Helena Ross, a cousin who boasted of her "blue blood" and looked practically white. They had ten children, cared for them well, kept a comfortable home, had a farm newspaper, and brought up their children to work on the theory that "a child which works won't steal." This family held itself rather aloof from the other Joneses; Helena had "some schooling," and was above average for the Wins.

Their oldest son fathered two illegitimate children with a Brown; the woman's mother would not allow them to marry because her daughter "had fits."

Their second child, a daughter, had light hair, blue eyes, and pink cheeks; she married another person with fair skin, a Nevin, who was supposedly Irish.

Child number three was a son. He had straight black hair, was considered handsome, and "gave the appearance of being of Italian origin." He was known as "the most normal boy of the Win area," but was never permitted to attend school beyond a profunctory appearance now and then. However, he reportedly worked hard, had a keen sense of humor, and eventually joined the Navy.

Child number four was a girl. She attended school for some years, but never passed the second grade. Later she became "sexually promiscuous" through associations at her married sister's home.

The other children of this family generally follow the same pattern. In this extensive study of the Indian Jones tribe, one finds an emphasis on slow learning, a lack of morals, illegitimacy, and intermarriage.

## General Comments—The Win Population

In 1926 the Win population was 658; 566 of these belonged to the Brown-Jones families, with the common ancestor, Thomas. However it included the names Brown, Jones, Lane, Black, Johnson, Long, and Hall, plus 84 people of "out-blood" who had married into the network here and there. Thirty-five of the eighty-four were classified as white, forty-nine as "colored" (which included those of Indian, black, and mixed blood). Four blacks had married into the family, three of whom were considered full-blooded.

## Fecundity

Fecundity (fertility) in the Win group was high. There were few women who had no children. Generation five had a rate of 4.83 children for each child-bearing female [1926], and this figure was expected to go higher. Generation four had a rate of 5.58 children per female, and this generation was (by the time of the study) practically past child-bearing age. There were only fourteen known women out of 139 who were barren among those who had ceased reproduction; this was approximately ten percent of the group.

## Consanguinity

Consanguinity (having the same parent or ancestor) ran as high as fifty percent. Records show that about half the matings of the Wins had been into the family itself. In generation five, 58.6 percent were back in the family. Generation six was still mating in 1926, and about 37 percent of the matings were consanguineous. The social barriers erected against the Wins in earlier times and continued through the present (1926) by the whites and blacks of Ab County were a factor forcing the Wins to mate within their own group. Such intermarriage was not a thing of their own choosing, for many considered it a social asset to be married to a white person, or even someone lighter than oneself.

Some few "stray men" mated outside the family here and there, usually with females "from poor stock mentally."

## Illegitimacy

A tabulation of births in the Win group according to legitimacy gives a general figure of 20 percent illegitimate. However, there were quite a number of women among the Wins who were known to have been sexually promiscuous. In fact, it has been said by members of one particular generation that only two women of that entire generation knew who the fathers of their children actually were. This may have been an exaggeration, however, since many Win women in later marriages were known to have been faithful to their husbands.

## Sexual Mores

In generation four, much promiscuity was found among both men and women. Five women had illegitimate children when single and without visible means of support for either themselves or their offspring. A few white men of Ab County regularly visited Win country for purposes of illicit relationships with Win women, and there were many illicit relationships between Win men and women themselves. Some said that practically all the women were amoral before marriage, and it was also said that many marriages were the direct result of premarital pregnancy. In some cases, men and women lived together for years and were faithful to each other without marriage, but later married after their children grew older.

Many factors seem to contribute to the lack of morals among the Wins. Living conditions in particular seem to have led to sexual familiarity. Many Win families exist in one room; few have more than two rooms in which to house sometimes large families. There seems to have been little restraint on the part of the adults, and the girls become ''boy-crazy'' at the ages of nine, ten, and eleven. ''A feeble-minded boy of twelve, with a mental age of six, told the researchers all about the illegitimate children of one of the Win women, including who the fathers were, and did so in a perfectly nonchalant manner.''

Intemperance and drunkenness were not found to any great extent among the Wins. Physicians in Ab County reported little or no venereal disease among them. Tuberculosis cases in the group in 1920 were 23 from a population of 658; this included 18 deaths and 5 suspected cases. Pure-blood Indians and blacks were said to be susceptible to the disease.

## Education

After the Civil War the Wins were given a chance to attend the schools for blacks, but not for whites. Claiming Indian blood, they refused to go to school at all. The result was that many received no education.

About 1895 Ab County started a school for the Indians with a white teacher. It lasted about ten years. A number of Wins attended irregularly, usually stopping in the fall to help on the farm. Few did even average work in school.

Before the turn of the century, schools were placed under the joint control of church missions and county authorities. In the course of nearly thirty years of ''schooling,'' not one Win was ever sufficiently educated to become a teacher and take on a leadership role among the Win people. The greater number did not go beyond the third grade. A few reached the fifth, and two the seventh. Only one (Helena Ross Jones) had papers to read in the home.

## Classification

The United States Census in earlier years classified the Wins as "free persons of color." As late as 1910, all were still listed as "colored" except for seven.

In 1920 all the Wins slipped by an unwary census enumerator, and the entire group was classified as "Indian." (The Indian population thus increased a hundredfold in a decade.)

If the census was not reliable, neither could one rely on marriage records. In greater Ab County prior to 1900, everyone except whites was listed as "colored." (For example, in 1888 Alphonse Brown and Belle Jones, both Indian-white, were listed as "colored"; yet two of their children, Antonio and Dean, were later listed as "white." In 1902, Ulysses and Helena Jones—he Indian and black, she Indian and white, were both given license as white, yet one of their children was married as "Indian.")

In 1924, the Virginia Legislature passed an act known as the Virginia Racial Integrity Law in which "the term 'white person' shall apply only to the person who has no trace whatsoever of any blood other than Caucasian; but persons who have one-sixteenth or less blood of the American Indian, and have no other non-Caucasic blood, shall be deemed white."

Already embodied in the state law was the clause: "Every person having one-sixteenth or more Negro blood shall be deemed a colored person." And: "Every person not a colored person, having one-fourth or more Indian blood, shall be deemed an Indian."

# Chapter Four
## OTHER MIXED AREAS

### On Top of the Blue Ridge

In this chapter we continue our notes on the Estabrook and McDougle study, *Mongrel Virginians.*

"On top of the Blue Ridge in Ad County, Virginia, at Paint Creek, is a group of red-skinned people who have long considered themselves white, although separated from [whites] socially." In 1926 this group numbered approximately 300. Physically, most of them looked like Indians with high cheekbones, reddish complexions, and straight black hair. The rest show the physical characteristics of blacks, particularly their curly hair and flat noses. The general light color of their skin indicates the presence of some white blood.

Prior to the Civil War several of these people claimed Indian descent. They lived on top of the Blue Ridge even before the Revolutionary War. Some of them, notably the Williams and Hammond families, still had land grant papers in their possession as late as 1920. Even Governor Spotswood of colonial days is reported to have seen members of this group when he passed through the Blue Ridge with his "Knights of the Golden Horseshoe."

Ad County was a battleground for the Indians, and some have said that many of these people were Iroquois who remained there after the battles, but others have questioned this recollection.

The Blue Ridge peoples were given schools in 1912. At that time their living standards were low. Many were lazy and shiftless; others were moonshiners. Later on, their income was augmented by cutting crossties for a lumber company.

There was no doubt about the presence of black blood in these Indian-whites, even though they denied it. Matings took place between them and the Wins, the whites in the valley, and each other.

## Smithtown—Ab County, Virginia

On the extreme western edge of Ab County, close to the foothills of the Blue Ridge, is Smithtown. About fifteen families of "Smiths" live there, all descended from Fred Smith, an Indian who settled in the area sometime around 1800.

Reputable people around the region said that there was an admixture of blacks with the Smiths in past years. White blood is also acknowledged. Black blood is evident in such characteristics as: kinky hair, flat noses and thick lips. However, the hair texture in many cases was soft and brown, the skin olive or white, sometimes with reddish copper showing through.

The illegitimacy rate was high, sexual mores very loose, and the paternity of many unknown. A few children showed a fair degree of intelligence, but school facilities were generally poor because of the inaccessibility of the area. The teacher [in 1926] was one of the Smiths, and she had the equivalent of a fifth-grade education.

Smithtown was located a good ten miles from a graded road. Tobacco was the only money crop. Most of the members of this group were tenants and were quite poor.

## Ag County, Virginia

In Ag County were scattered families with Indian-white blood. Some came from Ab County groups, and others were of unknown origin. These were all individual families; there were no group areas, as with the Wins or the people of Smithtown.

## Am County, Virginia

Near the town of "Polo" in Am County are several hundred Indians who are separated entirely from the local whites in social intercourse. Some admixture of the original Indian stock with both whites and blacks has been reported. These people nevertheless claim to be Indians, and as such have special schools for their children.

## Weromos

The Weremos live in "Rob and Plumb" counties; they are Indians who probably descended from the Powhatan tribe. They live on 800 acres of land ceded to them by the Colonial Assembly. Around 1920 their tribe numbered 110. Authorities in American ethnology agreed that their blood had become somewhat "tainted," especially by black blood. The estimate of its purity runs all the way from one-sixteenth to three-fourths. Around 1920, matings with blacks were forbidden by tribal rules.

Their government seems to be that of a pure democracy. A chief council of four is elected, and land is held in common. The state of Virginia supplies the teachers for a free school on the reservation.

## Groups of Delaware and Maryland

The authors of this study believe that there are groups of people near Stanton, Delaware, who have an Indian-black mixture, and who have mixed with whites as well. Others say that there is also an Indian-black mixture in the southern part of Maryland, and some mixing with whites there, as well. Whether these are extensions of the Blue Ridge and Piedmont groups is not known. They may well be what Mr. W.H. Gilbert of the Library of Congress once described as "Wesorts," a group much like the Melungeons.

## North Carolina

The authors of *Mongrel Virginians* also mention "Robin County, North Carolina," which has probably been discussed as "Robeson County" in other places in these notes. They describe it as a region that was the home of approximately 10,000 Indians [in 1926] called the "Rivers" (the Lumbees). The Rivers' history is left in doubt, but some descent is claimed from the Captain John White colony left on "Cremo" Island (Roanoke).

Some of the Indians of Robin County have stated that French immigrants settled the area as early as 1690, and that they (the French) came in contact with a mixed race they named "Mero" (Melungeons).

The Rivers Indians also say that a study of the names in the colony of John White shows forty percent of the family names in the Indian colony can be be found in the Rivers of Robin County. In the 1920s, this group spread out into "Norton" County, South Carolina, just across the line. About 3000 of them live there.

Their main crop was cotton, and corn was raised to feed large herds of hogs. With a few men who were in business in the town of "Slater," they were mostly "tillers of the soil."

There were many physical characteristics among them: long straight hair, kinky, curly, and soft hair. Skin colors varied from blue-black through copper-red, yellow, and white. With the lighter skins one would find blue or hazel eyes. All of them seemed sensitive to the idea that there could have been some black admixture among them; this attitude seemed to have developed after 1835 when an act of the North Carolina Legislature classified them all as "colored."

Prior to 1925, school authorities seem to have made special efforts to keep blacks out of the area, and little or no admixture seems to have taken place in the previous fifty years. However, the effects of past admixtures showed up in "nappy and curly heads," flat noses, thick lips, and yellow complexions.

Skin color seemed to play little part in intelligence levels. Some of the very dark members appeared to have the greater mental capacity.

One family, the "Prices," seemed to be a "high grade" of people. They had a noticeable red color that was constant throughout their family. These same Prices were related to the Price gang of criminals who murdered and robbed immediately after the Civil War.

The "Havens," "Keiths," "Duncans," and "Prices" were the aristocrats of the Rivers. Some had graduated from college. One Price was a graduate of the Johns Hopkins Medical School. "Stephen Wall," ex-senator from Mississippi, was born in Robin County, and is from this tribe. (He graduated from Oberlin College, and later moved to Mississippi.)

"Stanley Newcomb" was educated at Howard University and became a lawyer. Later he was in the State Legislature and became dean of a well known college. He was always classified as "colored."

In 1885, a local historian made a study of the group and concluded that they were descendants of the John White colony and the friendly tribe who had befriended those early explorers. This historian helped secure passage of an act by the North Carolina Legislature providing schools for them; the same legislature voided marriages between them and persons of black descent.

Many of these Indians have gone to other places, have passed for white, and married whites.

Illegitimacy is no greater among this group than in the general population of the area. There is not an exceptionally large amount of crime among the Rivers group, although they do seem capable of harboring grudges for a long time. Temperamentally, they show little resemblance to blacks.

## South Carolina

In "Norton" County, South Carolina, there are about 3000 of the above-mentioned Rivers. The state has [by 1926] taken no interest in them, and they have no special classification. Until sometime between 1910 and 1920 they either had to attend black schools or none at all. There was much admixture with blacks. All are poor tenant farmers considered by their white neighbors to be "improvident, unindustrious and immoral."

The northwestern corner of the above county also had a group of people known as the "Cheek" (probably a branch of the Creek) Indians, whose physical characteristics varied from black, straight hair, deep brown eyes, and dark red skin, to kinky hair, soft brown hair, and light skin with the red showing through. Many of them owned their own land, were traders, and had better homes. They were "interested in each other's business  and would trade horses and even tell lies for each other."

Among the "lower classes" of both these groups there was some "licentiousness." Special schools were provided for them. County authorities thought they ranked well with white pupils when they had competent teachers. About eight or ten had attended college. The Cheeks claimed they were directly descended from the Indian tribe of that name which lived in the area in colonial times. Their claim (seems to be) well authenticated, although there has obviously been considerable mixing with both blacks and whites.

## Another South Carolina Group

In a sandhill section of "Rand" County, South Carolina, the authors say that there lives a feeble-minded group of people said to have been of mixed red-black-white stock. Some members of this group have strong black characteristics, while others are practically white. Some relationships that brought this about could be worked out, while others were impossible to discern. A full-blooded Chinaman had mated into the group early on, complicating matters immensely.

This group may have a connection with the so-called "Brass Ankles" of South Carolina.

## Meros

Estabrook and McDougle also describe a mixed group of people living in southwestern Virginia and eastern Tennessee as "Meros." These could be none other than the Melungeons. They are described as "generally dark in color, some with straight hair, some with curly...they are quite numerous, and are an offshoot of the Rivers; it is considered a triple mixture."

# Chapter Five
## OTHER KINDRED TRIBES

The following summaries were compiled by Mr. W.H. Gilbert of the Government and General Research Group, Library of Congress, Washington. The information quoted in this section first appeared in a 1968 pamphlet by Mr. Gilbert entitled "Race, Cultural Groups." Much is recorded here which suggests a similarity between all the groups; I have also included Mr. Gilbert's data on the Melungeons themselves.

### The "Jackson Whites" of New Jersey and New York

"Jackson Whites" is a name said to be derived from "Jackson and White," which are common surnames. The same derivation is possible from "Jacks and Whites," terms once used for Negroes and Caucasians. Still another possibility is that Jackson was a man who imported some of the ancestors of the Jackson Whites during the Revolutionary War. (The so-called "blue-eyed Negroes" live in one part of this area, and are said to be a race apart from the rest.) The numbers of Jackson Whites are estimated to be "upwards of 500."

Location: Orange and Rockland counties in New York; Morris and Passaic Counties in New Jersey.

Organization: Family groups only. Some family names are: Casalony, Cisco, De Great, De Wies, Mann, Van Dunk, etc.

Environment and Economy: They are mainly a hill people of the Ramapo Hills. They raise a few crops at favorable spots and hunt. Many have migrated to the lowlands and to industrial mining areas.

Physique: In some areas pure white types are found, while in other areas "Negroid" types dominate. In still other areas Indian-mixed types seem predominant. Albinism and deformation does occur.

Intermarriage: Due to environmental limitations, this has been high.

Religion: Protestant in the main. Presbyterians have had a mission among them.

Schools: In New Jersey, some have attended white schools. No data on this subject is available from New York. Members of this group tend to concentrate in a few schools.

Cultural Peculiarities: Differences and oddities in dialect; home-made utensils; folklore.

Social Status: Regarded as "colored" by white neighbors.

History: Tradition holds that they derived from Tuscarora and Munsee Indians, Hessians, English, Negroes from the West Indies, etc. First described by Frank G. Speck of Park Ridge, New Jersey, in 1911.

## The Moors and Nanticokes of Delaware and New Jersey

The name "Moor" traditionally derived from shipwrecked Moorish sailors.

Location: Around Millsboro in Sussex County, Delaware, and at Bridgeton, in Cumberland County in southern New Jersey. The Moors number about 500 in Delaware, the Nanticokes about 700 in all areas.

Organization: Nanticokes are incorporated into groups larger than the family. Moors have no organization other than the family.

(a) Moor family names are: Carney (or Corney), Carver, Coker, Dean, Durham, Hansley (or Hansor), Hughes, Morgan, Mosley, Munce, Reed, Ridgeway, Sammon, Seeney.

(b) Nanticoke names are: Bumberry, Burke, Burton, Clarke, Cormeans, Coursey, Davis, Drain, Hansor, Harmon, Hill, Jackson, Kimmey, Layton, Miller, Morris, Moseley, Newton, Norwood, Reed, Ridgeway, Rodgers, Sockum, Street, Thomas, Thompson, Walker and Wright.

Environment: Originally both groups may have been swamp hunters and fishermen; now [in the 1940s] they are truck farmers.

Physique: Indian, black and white types occur. Drooped eyelids are inherited in one family strain.

Intermarriage: Customary.

Religion: Protestant. Some sections among the Nanticokes have their own churches.

Schools: Moors attend black schools. Nanticokes have their own schools, with teacher salaries paid by the state.

Cultural Peculiarities: Utensils and implements formerly made locally by the Nanticokes. These people also have their own medicines and folklore.

Social status: Uncertain.

History: The Nanticokes were first noticed about 1889; the Moors about 1895.

## The "Red Bones" of Louisiana

The term "Red Bone" apparently derived from the French *Os Rouge* which was used to describe persons of partly Indian blood. The Red Bones were also called "Houmas" along the coast, and "Sabines" farther west. In the parish of Natchitoches, they are called the "Cane River Mulattoes."

Location: The parishes of Natchitoches, Vernon, Calcasieu, Terrebonne, La Fourche, and St. Tammany.

Mr. Gilbert provides no further data on this group.

## The Melungeons

The name of this group is said to derive from the French *Melange,* meaning *mixed;* or from *Melan,* from the Greek word meaning *black.* Some migrated from the areas below to southeastern Kentucky, and a few to Blountstown, Florida, just west of Tallahassee. It is also possible that some went westward to the Ozarks. Their numbers are estimated to be between five and ten thousand, and they have a high birth rate.

Location:

(a) Original center of dispersal was probably Newman's Ridge in Hancock County, Tennessee. From there they spread to other Tennessee counties, including Cocke, Davidson, Franklin, Grundy, Hamilton, Hawkins, Knox, Marion, Meigs, Morgan, Overton, Rhea, Roane, Sullivan, White, Wilson, Bledsoe, and Van Buren.

(b) In southwest Virginia: Giles, Lee, Russell, Scott, Washington, and Wine.

Organization: Family groups only. Some original family names are Collins, Gibson (or Gipson), Goins, Mullins (or Mellons), Bolen, Denham, Freeman, Gann, Gorvens, Graham, Noel, Piniore, Sexton, Wright.

Environment and Economy: Originally, they were pioneer cultivators in the Appalachian Valley lowlands, but are said to have been driven to the ridges by white settlers. They currently live along Newman's

Ridge, and on Clinch Mountain, Copper Ridge, and the Cumberland Range in eastern Tennessee.

Means of livelihood: Originally hunting, fishing, ginseng-root gathering, herb-gathering, charcoal-burning. In earlier years: riverboat carriage and livestock driving. Later: tenant farming, small land owning, coal mining. Apparently they also did work in basketry, chair making, and cooperage (making or repairing barrels, casks, etc.).

Dwellings: Crude; sometimes in the sides of cliffs. They often prefer to live in wild, unfrequented hill country.

Physique: Characteristically, their features range between Indian, white, and occasional Negroid types. Their stoic endurance of out-of-doors life is notable.

Intermarriage: Originally they married only within the group, but considerable outside marriage with whites has occurred in recent years.

Religion: Presbyterians have had missions among them for many years, notably at Vardy and Sycamore (Sneedville Post Office), in Tennessee. Some are Baptists. Hymns that are peculiar to some mountain sects are sung.

Schools: They attended white schools in Franklin, Marion, and Rhea Counties in Tennessee, but only after winning lawsuits regarding their racial classification. In southwest Virginia they attended white schools if they went to school at all. Most are illiterate.

Military Draft Status: Illiteracy is said to be a hindrance to their military service in some places.

Voting and Civil Rights: They were disenfranchised in Tennessee by the Constitution of 1834 [which labelled them "free persons of color" and effectively barred them from owning land]; they have voted since the Civil War, primarily for Republican candidates. During the 1960s more of them have lined up with Democrats, however.

Relief: They were given food and clothing in Virginia during the depression of the 1930s.

Cultural Peculiarities: A belief in magic and folklore seems important to them.

Social Status: [Mr. Gilbert states that they are said to approximate white social status in many areas. However, I believe this would be valid only if he is referring to the poorer whites.]

History: There are several theories of origin. Some believe they are derived from the Croatans; others say they come from Portuguese,

Negro, Moorish, and English ancestries. They appeared in east Tennessee soon after the American Revolution. Their first modern notice under the name ''Melungeon'' was about 1889.

# Chapter Six
## THEORIES, TRADITIONS, AND STATISTICS

Mr. Bruce Crawford, in his *Coalfield Progress* of July 11, 1940, said Rankin's Ferry at Chattanooga, Tennessee, was once operated by a family of Melungeons, and that Admiral Farragut, of naval fame during the Civil War, was a Melungeon. Crawford passed on the latter information as pure tradition. The *Tennessee Conservationist* once mentioned the name of a Melungeon family called Dungee who kept a toll gate on the Charlotte Pike around the time of the Civil War.

The Portuguese tradition seems to persist in connection with the Melungeons much more strongly than even that of the Lost Colony. A few years ago your author, who had just published a brief article on the Melungeons, received a query from a woman living in another state. She was concerned about an ancestor by the name of Sidebottom, whom she thought to be of Portuguese ancestry. Since I am an amateur genealogist, her comments challenged me, but after digging for a time (and even excavating a bit), I could only come up with the early colonial Sidebottoms, who must have been English and slaveholders.

A quotation from an article written by Mrs. Eliza N. Heiskell of Memphis appeared in an issue of the *Arkansas Gazette* in 1912. She gave the tradition of a Portuguese ship and a mutiny with successful mutineers beaching their vessel on the North Carolina coast, then making a rapid retreat to the mountains, which protected them from their enemies.

The late John Netherland of Tennessee, Mrs. Heiskell's father (and an opponent of Isham G. Harris for the Tennessee governorship in 1859), obtained the right of citizenship for the Melungeons, and for years they revered his memory somewhat like others revere the memory of a patron saint. Mrs. Heiskell has described the Melungeons as having been like Irish peasants, in that one of their principal recreations was telling and hearing stories of hunting adventures and neighborhood fights. She said that they also had many superstitions, particularly concerning the power of the moon  and the reality of "haints."

## "A Caste Distinction"

Since the Tennessee Constitutional Convention of 1834 classified the Melungeons as "free persons of color," they were not allowed to testify in court in any case involving a Caucasian. This opened the way for unscrupulous and covetous settlers to move in on their flat land, while they retired to remote ridges where no court cases could perturb them. They lived in rude log shacks, planted corn, traded ginseng and other herb roots, hunted, fished, and even made whiskey.

People still living in Blackwater Valley, Virginia, and in Sneedville and Kyle's Ford in Tennessee, can remember Mahala Mullins (also called "Big Haley"), a Melungeon of immense proportions. I heard her story

from my father, who grew up on Blackwater Creek. As a young man, he often visited Sneedville, the county seat of Hancock County, Tennessee, by way of Newman's Ridge. "Big Haley," who lived on the Virginia-Tennessee line, had grown so obese that she never left her house; all day long she sat in a doorway and sold whiskey to travelers.

When Virginia Law Officers approached to discuss the matter with her, she simply got up and waddled over to the Tennessee side of her cabin; and if the Tennessee authorities showed up, she moved to the Virginia side.

All this was probably unnecessary, since Mahala was said to have weighed between six and seven hundred pounds and could not have been gotten to court even if she had been arrested. When she died, it was even difficult to get her to her grave. While there are different versions of that operation (my parents, for example, once told me that the chimney was removed in order to make a hole big enough to get her out of her house), a native of Blackwater Valley told me that one of the four walls of the house had to be torn down to move her. The huge homemade bed upon which she slept (and died) was converted to a makeshift coffin, in which she was carried to her final resting place.

Dr. Swan M. Burnett, an east Tennessee physician, made numerous notes on the Melungeons for the Anthropological Society in Washington, D.C., which he presented in 1889. It appears that in the doctor's family, the Melungeons were considered fearful creatures; when he was a child, they were the "bogey man."

Dr. Burnett said that when he grew older and began the practice of medicine, he found the awe-inspiring Melungeons to be somewhat like other people, but with definite peculiarities. They were not only different from the blacks, both slave and free, but from the Indians and whites as well; this difference set them apart from both whites and blacks, much as the whites and blacks were themselves separated. They deeply resented the name "Melungeon" given them by whites, and proudly called themselves Portuguese.

According to Dr. Burnett, an old man named Sol Collins of Hancock County, Tennessee, claimed that his father fought in the Revolutionary War. In describing this family, Dr. Burnett said:

> "They were generally known as Collinses, etc., and, due to [certain] caste restrictions, they have not recently intermarried with Negroes or Indians. They were held by whites to be a mixed race, with at least a modicum of Negro blood. There was at least one record in which the matter was brought before the courts.

> "It was before the Civil War, during the period of slavery, that the right of a number of people in this group to vote was questioned.

The matter was finally carried before a jury, where the question was decided by an examination of the feet. One...was found sufficiently flat-footed to deprive him of the right of suffrage. The other four or five were judged to possess enough white blood to be allowed to vote. Colonel John Netherland, a prominent local lawyer [mentioned previously], defended them.''

Dr. Burnett also said that among the ''more thoughtful'' people there was a ''disposition'' to give credence to the Melungeons' claim that they were a distinct race. A few people inclined toward the Portuguese theory, some saying the Melungeons were Gypsies, with some of the later families intermingling with blacks, or Indians, or both.

''They are dark, but different from the mulatto, with either straight or wavy hair, and some have cheek bones almost as high as the Indians.

''The men are usually large, straight, and fine looking, but they do not stand very high in the community. Their reputation for truthfulness and honesty is not to be envied. However, there are individual exceptions.''

### Another Role for the Melungeons

From the *History of Tennessee and the Tennesseans,* published in 1913 by W.T. Hale and Dixon L. Merritt (Volume I, pp. 8, 179-80), we find another facet of the Melungeons:

''From time immemorial they have been counterfeiters of gold and silver and, strange to say, their money contained more of the precious metals per coin than that minted by the government. At one time during my recollection these coins passed without question. There is a legend that their silver came from Straight Creek, a tributary of the Cumberland River which flows into that stream at Cumberland Ford (now Pineville, Kentucky). Ruins of ancient furnaces are still to be seen along the banks of Straight Creek, but have not been used within the memory of anyone living. A family named Mullins were the makers of the silver money in that section. The Beckler gold dollars were coined in North Carolina, and some of these coins are yet extant, preserved as curiosities. They were of native gold made by a family named Beckler, and were called 'Becklers.'

"The reference to the gold and silver coins of the Melungeons suggests [the same story a man named] Adair told of silver in east Tennessee in a history of the Indians published in London in 1775.

"Within twenty miles of Fort Loudon the silver mines are so rich that, by digging about ten yards deep, some desperate vagrants found at sundry times so much rich ore as to enable them to counterfeit dollars to a great amount, a horse-load of which was detected in passing for purchase of Negroes at Augusta."

Were these "desperate vagrants" the people we call Melungeons?

### Enter Miss Dromgoole

Toward the end of the 1800s a Nashville writer and poetess, Miss Will Allen Dromgoole, made an extensive, first-hand study of the Melungeons. She spent months living among them in their homes on Newman's Ridge, on the border of Hancock County in Tennessee where it meets Virginia. (Interestingly enough, the origin of "Newman" may be from "new man," a term coined because it seemed to describe this ridge's strange inhabitants.) Miss Dromgoole reported her impressions and conclusions in the *Arena Magazine,* published in Boston in 1891.

She described many strange facets of Melungeon life, some of which she thought might have indicated a Latin origin. Miss Dromgoole was puzzled by an unusual veneration for the Christian cross, in view of the fact that most other people who lived in the area, if religious at all, were more inclined toward the "shouting," emotional type of Protestantism, seldom using the cross as a symbol in their services. She also mentioned the strange custom the Melungeons had of burying their dead above the ground in small token houses over the graves, "somewhat as Spanish and Indian Catholics, or Alaskan Indian converts to Creek Catholocism had a custom of doing...."

Some historians have said that they question whether such token houses ever existed, casting doubt as to Miss Dromgoole's accuracy; however, a few years ago I was giving a paper on the Melungeons at a regional meeting of a sociological and historical group, and a man from the audience told me that there were such graves in Scott County, Virginia, even as we spoke. All I can say personally is that I have seen small houses built over Melungeons' graves, but only after the body was in the ground.

Miss Dromgoole wrote that John A. McKinney of Hawkins County, Tennessee, was chairman of the committee of the Constitutional Convention of 1834 which handled matters affecting "free persons of color." McKinney held that this phrase was a code word for "Melungeon." Dromgoole believes that the amendment of the fundamental law of the state, denying them their oath as well as suffrage, rendered Melungeons desperate. She says:

"They betook themselves to the hills, where-they huddled together. They became a law unto themselves, a race distinct from several races inhabiting the state, and were soon a terror to the people of the foothills and valleys, swooping down and stealing their cattle, provisions, clothing, and furniture. In time they became, almost to a man, distillers of brandy."

Is there any better illustration, anywhere in the world, of the destructive, evil effect of codified prejudice?

At the outbreak of the Civil War a few Melungeons enlisted, but most are said to have remained on the ridges, caring for their stills and plundering the valleys. Miss Dromgoole stated that their mountains became a terror to travelers, and that it was not safe to cross Melungeon country until about 1885. I have never heard my father mention such dangers, but he was only a lad in 1885. I do recall stories by one of his contemporaries describing the amusing but polite and respectful manner in which a Melungeon child, sent to borrow something, would address a white neighbor:

"Pap sent m'down hyer t'see ef he c'd borry a chaw o' t'baccer fer Gran'pap."

With those who insisted that the Melungeons were mulattoes, Miss Dromgoole argued that a race of mulattoes could not exist as did Melungeons. She says:

"The Negro race goes from mulatto to quadroon, and from quadroon to octaroon, where it stops, for octaroon women bear no children."

She points out that in most Melungeon shacks live mothers, grandmothers, and sometimes great-grandmothers. She describes the Melungeons on Newman's Ridge as:

"possessing a striking resemblance to the Cherokee Indians, and that they were believed by many of their neighbors to have been a kind of half-breed Indians.

"Their complexion is reddish brown, totally unlike that of the mulatto...the women are small, below average height, with coal-black hair, black eyes, and high cheekbones."

She calls the hands of the Melungeon women "shapely," and adds that their feet were likewise, despite the fact that they often travel barefoot over rough mountain paths. She thought their features wholly unlike those of the Negro, except in cases where the two races cohabited, as was sometimes the case. On Newman's Ridge proper, she found only pure Melungeon stock; it was in the Blackwater Swamp and Big Sycamore Creek that the mixed races lived.

Some historians have said that the extinction of the Melungeon race has been so nearly complete that it is now known only in a few counties of east Tennessee. Others have said that the minute you cross the Hancock County line you see them; but they are evidently unaware of the settlement on Stone Mountain in Wise, and the High Knob area in Wise and Scott Counties of Virginia, in Lee County and other southwestern Virginia areas, and in eastern Kentucky.

The people on Newman's Ridge have been referred to as "Ridgmanites" or "pure Melungeons," while those among whom Negro blood has entered have been called "Blackwaters" from the Blackwater Swamps. Your author has not heard them labelled thusly, but I have heard my elders refer to them as "the Black Collinses and the other Collinses." Some of the Ridge group have used the name "Collinsworth." One man named "Bud" Collins married my father's step-sister; Bud was a banker at Sneedville, Tennessee, and reared a family of educated and useful citizens.

Miss Dromgoole published a second article in the same year in which she retracted many of her earlier statements about the Melungeons. She reversed some of her opinions of the race, which no longer seemed interesting or mysterious to her, possibly because of some unpleasant experience along the way. She also concluded that Octaroon women were not always barren after all; and she decided that Melungeons were not, in all cases, friendly, even using such words as "dirty," "thieving," and "decadent" to describe them.

In her later writings she claimed to have learned their real history, and proceeded to relate the most incredible story, which follows:

"Two wily Cherokees borrowed names of white settlers in

Virginia. They called themselves 'Vardy Collins' and 'Buck Gibson.' In a nearby forest Vardy supposedly covered Buck with a dark dye, or stain, and took him to a farmhouse belonging to one of the wealthier white citizens of the area, where he sold him as a 'likely nigger' for 300 dollars and a team of mules. With the loot he vanished into the forest. Meanwhile, 'Gibson' went to a stream and washed off the black stain and left the place a free man, denying any knowledge of a 'likely nigger.' Afterward he was said to have met Collins in the woods [where they] divided the loot and went their separate ways.''

She gives no authority whatsoever for this tale, and further states that:

''A Collins came to Newman's Ridge and reared a family by a wife whose ancestry was more vague than that of Cain's wife.''

A Vardy Collins was indeed listed in the 1830 Census of Hawkins County, Tennessee, parent county of Hancock.

Miss Dromgoole also told of an English trader named Mullins who came to Newman's Ridge and married one of the Collins daughters, and of a ''free or escaped Negro named Goins, [who] married another daughter'' and settled in the Blackwater Swamps. (Miss Dromgoole surely knew that such a marriage was not legal in either Tennessee or Virginia.) She added that a Portuguese named Denham arrived ''from somewhere'' and married another Collins daughter.

Miss Dromgoole goes on to list common surnames among the Melungeons. Included are Gorven, Gibbens, Bragans or Brogan. (The word ''brogan'' in this area has always been associated with a coarse, crudely made man's or boy's shoe.) She thought that the system of identifying each other in which (for example) the wife of Jack Collins was called ''Mary Jack,'' their daughter ''Sally Jack,'' their son ''Tom Jack'' was a custom original with the Melungeons, but the same system has been followed by non-Melungeon families in the area for generations. It was still in comman usage in my own community when I was a child.

Miss Dromgoole's final estimate of the Melungeons was evidently resented by those who were her subject. A few living citizens who were born and reared in Sneedville and Kyle's Ford in Hancock County before the 1890s can still recall a little jingle in which she was referred to as ''Miss Will Allen Damfool.''

## More Conjectures

Woodson Knight, a Kentucky writer and journalist, claimed in 1940 that there may have been a Welsh background for the Melungeons and suggested that those along the Clinch River might have descended from an early Welsh chieftain named Madoc, who, according to legend, sailed to the West in the days of the Roman Empire's decline. No proof was offered to support this legend.

Another theory has been advanced by James Aswell, a Tennessee history expert. He has said that a possible explanation for the Melungeons is an old story that Portuguese ships were plying the Caribbean as pirates at the time of the Portuguese revolt against Spain in 1685. As a means of disposing of unwanted crew members they sometimes marooned them on the Florida Keys, or even on the mainland of the North American continent. Some crews allegedly mutinied, and one of these may have burned its ship, attacked some small Indian villages ashore, taken the women, and fled westward to the mountains. Aswell thought it possible for them to have reached Hancock County, Tennessee, if their mutiny had taken place on the North Carolina coast. Obviously, this theory is imaginative.

### Locations and Statistics

In a column called "The Southwest Corner" published in the *Roanoke News,* Roanoke, Virginia, on February 25, 1934, Dr. Goodridge Wilson wrote the following:

"Uncle Sam's census tells us that there are now fifteen Indians living in southwest Virginia, or were in 1930. [This is] a rather meager representation for a race that once roamed in undisputed mastery over all this lonely domain, and which for near a half-century ferociously contested the white man's right to live anywhere within its borders. Small as it is, however, that representation is probably larger than most of us would suppose...but I have serious doubts about any of them being full-blooded aborigines.

"Three of the fifteen are reported as living in Bristol, two in Wise County, three in Lee, and seven in Giles. In 1920 there were nine reported in Giles and six in Lee, with no others reported in southwestern Virginia. A former resident of Giles tells me that there is in that county a family of marked Indian features, swarthy complexion and straight black hair. They claim to be Indians. They live in the Dismal region, a wild, mountainous section of western Giles where the environment invites a mode of life conforming, as near as modern conditions anywhere allow, to that of their primitive forebears.

"It would appear from the census figures that thirty-odd years ago Lee County had quite a colony of Indians, when the census assigned sixty-four to the county...a native of the county who knows it from one end to the other says that if any Indians have lived in it within recent decades he never heard of them. He thinks that those census Indians are 'Melungeons.'

"The origin of the Melungeons is shrouded in the mists of an uncertain past. They are socially and racially distinct from the blacks and whites around them, and are not classified as Indians. Some of them, I am told, live in the vicinity of Damascus in Washington County, Virginia, their forebears having squatted on the big survey, or Douglas Lands of Roosevelt connections. Many of them lived in sections of North Carolina, and a number inhabit Newman's Ridge, a long rugged line of...rocky hills lying between Clinch River and Powell Mountain, and running out of Scott, through Lee County, and far down into Tennessee. The thin soil of the region would seem incapable of supporting a population, but in the secluded hollows of its watercourses are clusters of crude cabins in which the Melungeons and their ancestors have lived since 'time immemorial' (as 'immemorial time' goes in this comparatively new land of ours).

"They have lived by hunting and fishing, digging roots and gathering herbs, burning charcoal, flat-boating on the Clinch, serving as herdsmen for droves of hogs, cattle, horses, mules, and sheep that were driven on foot from the hill pastures to distant markets. Since the passing of such opportunities, many have found employment in coal mining. Some of the more thrifty and intelligent, leaving their ancestral ridge homes, have become successful renters and small landowners in the better land areas. Some have been efficient in such trades as basket and chair making, and cooperage.

"Mr. Robert Gray, one of the last survivors of those who drove the great herds of cattle, horses, and mules from the mountains to the sea, says that the Melungeons were in much demand for this work, being expert handlers of the stock on long treks. He says, too, that quartering them at night was a difficult problem, because both the employers and the folks who entertained them along the way thought these people should be quartered and fed with the [blacks], an arrangement to which both Melungeons and [blacks] objected.

"They, themselves, disliked the term 'Melungeon.' The Newman's Ridge contingent prefer to be called 'Portuguese,' claiming descent from a band of Portuguese immigrants who, they say, settled Newman's Ridge about the time of the Revolution. Research, however, fails to produce any evidence of such Portuguese immigration; and such names as Collins and Sexton, common among them, are distinctly not of Latin flavor. They are of short, stocky build with black eyes, black (usually curly) hair, facial features sometimes of Indian, sometimes of Caucasian types. Albinos, pink-eyed and white-haired, are not uncommon among them. Castlewood in Russell County, Virginia, derives its name from an albino who wandered off from the settlements in Rockbridge County and took up with the Indians on Clinch River. He, like all albinos, was held in superstitious regard by the savages....

"Another theory of their origin is that they descended from the fringes of the Wilderness Road migration to Kentucky, weaklings who dropped off from their strenuous journey and took up their abode in the unclaimed and undesired lands of Newman's Ridge, where they intermarried with stray bands of Indians."
[It would be difficult to convince anyone who knows of the physical endurance of the Melungeons that they could have descended from weaklings of any race.]

"Mr. Gray says that when he was a boy some of the oldest of the clan told him that they were 'Croatoans,' survivors of the Indian tribe supposed to have destroyed or absorbed Sir Walter Raleigh's Lost Colony on Roanoke Island."

**Ramps**

In some sections the Melungeons have been called "ramps" by their white neighbors. This was particularly true in Wise County, Virginia, when your author resided there with her family in the 1930s. Nobody seemed to have an explanation for this name. Upon consulting Webster, I found that the word, as a noun, means "a leap; bond; ruffian; highwayman; rowdy woman (obsolete)."

In architecture it means "a concave bend; a talus of a fortification which serves as a sloping road between two levels."

In another reference, I found that it means *ramper-clamber* in the French; it is the root word of the German *raffin*. There is an area in east Tennessee which holds an annual "ramp festival." Once I ran across a definition that covered that one, too: a wild onion.

Still, we are left to our own conclusions as to why Melungeons have been called "ramps."

## An Old Timer Interviewed

A few years ago Mr. G.M. French, Jr., a native of southwestern Virginia who lives in Cheverly, Maryland, sent me his notes from an interview he had with one of the oldest residents of the Dungannon area of Scott County, Virginia, who lived on Copper Ridge.

The old timer was known as "Uncle Washington Osborne." In the interview, he said that the Melungeons began their migration to that part of Scott County, Virginia, and neighboring Wise County, about 1820. They came there, he said, in about equal numbers from Kentucky, Newman's Ridge, and the lower end of Lee County, Virginia. He added that a few had also come from North Carolina (and that is borne out by census records included as an appendix to these notes).

Uncle Washington Osborne also said that the first Collinses that came to his community were white. They came there from Kentucky, along with the Gibsons and Sextons. From Newman's Ridge came the Littons and Bollings (or Bowlings), Goins, and Baldwins. Some Melungeons, he said, had come from Letcher County, Kentucky, and they lived in great numbers near Neon and Whitesburg, at a place called "Lick Rock." He mentioned one Melungeon, "Uncle Poke Gibson," who came from Letcher County about 1820, and claimed to be "Portuguese Indian" (which I assume to mean a cross between the Portuguese and Indians).

Mr. Osborne referred to the Melungeons as "Melongo," which he defined as pure Portuguese. Quoting him in further detail:

"The Bollings, who are numerous in Scott County and Wise County, came from Newman's Ridge. They have all the features of the Indian race. Old Jack Bolling was the progenitor of the Scott County Bollings, and his people were strong, and spoke broken English."

(A local genealogist once told me that the Bollings of Wise County came from North Carolina, but they could well be a different branch of the family. There are hundreds, possibly even thousands, of Bollings who claim descent from the Indian Princess Pocahontas and her white husband, John Rolfe of early Jamestown history.)

In contrast to Miss Dromgoole's theories, this old-timer described the Goins family as having come from Blackwater, Tennessee, and "very near full Indian, a high-minded group of people" believed to have mixed with the white race. They settled among the whites of Scott County over the past 140 years.

Mr. Osborne also described the Sweeneys, who he said came from Blackwater, Tennessee, along with the Adkins, Lucases, and others. He says they were a "fighting tribe when in anger," but were otherwise "peaceful." He added that they were not as dark as others from that area, and that "nerve" was one of their outstanding traits (meaning they were not afraid of anything).

Another name he associated with the "Melongo" tribe was Lucas. He described their features as "large and massive," with ruddy cheeks. He thought they were descended from the "Portuguese-Indians." However, in the next sentence he stated that the Lucas name was of Irish origin.

Another name Mr. Osborne connected to Melungeons was Moore. He said that they came from Newman's Ridge to that area of Scott County as early as 1807. The progenitor of this Moore tribe was "Old Ethan Moore" (not the Ephriam Moore who later showed up on the Scott County census). He claimed Ethan was one-third "Portuguese-Indian." Then he added:

"Of course, the other two-thirds consisted of Irish and I don't know what. Ethan Moore had tolerable dark skin, broad cheekbones, very pretty eyes as black as a cat's, a nose three inches long, very flat and wide as a possum's. He spoke in an indistinct tone, since his words came out through his nose.

"Ethan Moore, a school-teacher, a man of knowledge and a brilliant mind, lived during the slave days, but kept no slaves, since he considered them too irresponsible to have on the place."

He described the Moores who were Ethan's descendants as people of good judgment, most of whom were very good-looking.

Mr. Osborne went on to say that some of the Melungeons came in from the North. [I believe he said this because they arrived in his area by way of Wise County, Virginia, and certain counties of eastern Kentucky.] He also separated them into the following seven groups:

(a) Purebred Indian groups such as Goins, Bolling, Sweeney, Adkins, and Minor.

(b) Indian groups from Blackwater who married into other "Melongo" tribes, such as Baldwin and Collins.

(c) Melongo groups from Kentucky, such as Collins, and Sexton.

(d) Portuguese Indian and whites from Newman's Ridge, such as Collins and Bolling.

(e) Portuguese Indians and whites such as Collins, from Blackwater; and Lucas, Sexton, and Gibson from Newman's Ridge.

(f) Portuguese Indians from Kentucky, such as Gibson.

(g) A pure-bred Indian group from Blackwater named Minor.

In speaking of the Minors, he said:

"The Minors are a fighting people and show more of the Indian than any other Indian group in Scott County. They claim to be of Portuguese-Indian stock. They are of large stature, tall, of dark complexion, and very strong. I believe the Minors are three-quarters Indian and one-quarter Portuguese. They are the type of people whose word is their bond. In Scott County some of them own large stock farms and have prospered."

One Samuel P. Sexton "verified" a story to Mr. Osborne that Sexton's aunt, Caroline Collins, had been told by her father, one Johnny Sexton, that the original Sexton who came to America came on a ship that carried Spanish bullion. Johnny Sexton himself supposedly came to Stone Mountain from eastern Virginia.

On October 18, 1947, a man named William L. Worden published an article in the *Saturday Evening Post* entitled "Sons of Legend," in which he gave an unusually vivid picture of the Melungeons in Hancock County, Tennessee. He also included some photographs of the tribe living here in 1947, with impressions of their homes, the Vardy Mission, and the Sneedville practitioner, one Dr. Doty, who sometimes visited your author's paternal grandmother in Lee County, Virginia, some fifty-odd years ago.

There are still Melungeons on Newman's Ridge in Hancock County, Hawkins County, and other counties in eastern Tennessee, eastern Kentucky, and southwestern Virginia. They were observed by Dr. E.T. Price, of the University of Cincinnati, when he wrote a dissertation on the subject around 1951. Others who have first-hand knowledge of the Melungeons of Hancock County, Tennessee, are: Mr. Delmar Wallen, of Kingsport, Tennessee, and Mr. Hampton Osborne of Clintwood, Virginia (the latter being a native of the Blackwater area in Lee County, Virginia).

The present-day Melungeons are largely farmers or tenants, but some have been miners. Most of them are indifferent to schools, with a probable exception of the mission school at Vardy, Tennessee. A few years ago I discussed the Melungeons with Dr. Ralph Clark of East Tennessee State University at Johnson City, Tennessee. He has visited the Vardy Mission and observed the Melungeons there. A few of them (or those with some Melungeon blood) have gone to church colleges, but there seems to be no record of any having graduated.

The Reverend Chester F. Leonard of the Vardy Mission made this statement: "The group is so intermingled that one cannot be sure of a typical specimen."

# Chapter Seven
## THE MELUNGEONS AS I SAW THEM

**1969**

Now to record some of my own impressions of the Melungeon families that I have known. In my youth I saw them in their homes and occasionally at school, and in later years some of them were my pupils. Were they unkept and unsanitary? Yes, many of them, but not consciously so. They labored efficiently on our farms, particularly when it came to "clearing new ground," or caring for livestock. They frequently worked, sat, or ate their meals in our homes, and even though it was sometimes necessary to go scurrying off for a cuspidor, or open a window, we had no occasion to doubt their loyalty or honesty. They usually married their kin. Their morals were not inferior to those of some of their white neighbors. I recall no illegitimate children among our own tenants. Some of them were quite religious.

Sometime around 1909 a couple named "Jassie and Sary," with their brood of seven, moved into a shack that stood in a small clearing between two rocky "thickets." Jassie was probably in his middle teens, muscular and sturdily built. He resembled both parents (who resembled each other); they had coarse tan skin, dark thick hair (Jassie's was somewhat curly), and teeth yellowed by chewing tobacco. However, it has been noted that decayed teeth were rare among this group.

"Gilly," the next son, was not too different from neighborhood boys, except for his facial features. His skin was of a lighter shade and smoother texture than those of his parents. His eyes were gray, his hair brown and slightly curly. The local boys referred to him as "Gilly Possum" because of the perpetual grin he wore. My mother succeeded for a short time in coaxing Gilly to attend Sunday School. The highlight of the summer attendance was a well-planned Children's Day program for the little rural church in which every child was expected to

participate. So Gilly was given a "role" in the program. On Saturday before the Sunday program, Mother gave Gilly one of my brother's old suits that he had outgrown, to wear for the occasion.

Early on Sunday morning Gilly showed up in the suit wearing his usual grin, but neither suit nor grin could deceive my mother. She filled a basin with warm water, unbuttoned his shirt collar, rolled up his sleeves, and began scrubbing him with homemade soap. Then she combed his hair and put a tie on him. Beaming, Gilly sauntered over to the little church. and later went through his recitation with smiling enthusiasm. That afternoon he tried to return the suit and tie, but mother told him they were his to keep.

There were younger children among the Melungeons who frequently ran about in winter with bare feet, which seemed to do them little harm. It was not unusual during the summer months to see them running about without any clothing on at all.

In a "sag" on the hillside above Jassie and Sary was a small log cabin with a lean-to kitchen. Jassie's brother, Creed, lived there with Lucy and Randy, his motherless children, and his aging father, Josiah. Creed

was even smaller than Jassie; he had black hair and eyes. His appearance was probably explained by the fact that he had married a girl outside the Melungeon tribe. She had been small and frail, but also rather pretty, as I vaguely remember. Her neighbors once described her to me as a "neat housekeeper," but apparently the mode of life among the hardy Melungeons was too much for her. She died soon after the birth of her third child, a boy; he was taken by a white neighbor, adopted, given affectionate care, and sent to school. His name was Charlie.

Charlie ran into problems at school. He was unduly sensitive, and resented being called a "Melungeon" by his classmates, as he invariably was. They often taunted him in order to "see the fire flash from his eyes," as an acquaintance of mine once put it. Charlie was also unable to resist tobacco.

After completing grammar school he dropped out of school and eventually married the daughter of a white farm tenant. On visits home in later years, I learned that he had followed the traditional pattern of his father's family: an indifference to schooling. After the attack on Pearl Harbor in 1941, he was drafted and lost his life in the service of the country.

Like Charlie, the Melungeons in our area cared little for education. When there appeared to be a lack of clothing, a charitable teacher would sometimes give the children new dresses or shirts to inspire and encourage them; but aside from Charlie, I do not recall one that was

ever promoted beyond the third grade. I doubt if Jassie could write his own name, but he knew a number of old ballads from memory, and enjoyed entertaining neighbors at corn-huskings and bean-strings. He had one "ditty" that he would sing while walking about the farm:

"Craw-fish! Craw-fish! You'd better go deep!
Or I'll eat you 'fore I sleep!"

Early every spring, while the men were logging or clearing new ground, the women and children were often seen gathering a fuzzy green plant growing alongside clear streams. They called it "bear's lettuce," and ate it raw, adding only salt. They also picked pails full of "wild sallet" (greens). "Sallet" consisted of poke, narrow dock, crow's foot, cress, lamb's quarters, and many other plants known to be edible. They usually cooked them with a piece of salt bacon and ate them with hard corn "pone" (bread) baked in a dutch oven in an open fireplace, or in a small "step-stove." Corn-meal mush was one of their favorite cold weather foods. I can recall passing by their shacks on my way to the apple orchard or to drive home the cows; once while it was raining I stopped and, with fascination, watched Jassie prepare their evening meal. This consisted of stirring mush in a big black metal pot, using a wooden spade.

On Saturday evenings the men and boys often went fishing. They seldom carried fishing poles or lines and hooks with them. Instead, they waded into the stream shoes and all, and started searching with their fingers for fish hidden under stones and shelving banks. They nearly always caught some fish, which they strung onto a pliable willow twig. They tied the twig to an overhanging bush with the fish dangling in the water until the fishermen were ready to go home, or to another fishing site. They seemed to know just where the fish were hiding.

On Sundays they visited with relatives who lived up and down the valley, or over on another ridge. When crowds came to the little community church for special events and brought baskets of food to be served on the grounds, the Melungeons turned out full force. They seemed to enjoy community gatherings, particularly the men. When there was a community Christmas tree, there was always a provision for giving gifts to the poor. The men sometimes participated by buying small gifts at the crossroads store and hanging them on the tree for their landlords' wives and daughters.

Josiah, an old man in his seventies, exemplifies Melungeon behavior amongst many elderly. At his age he was able to read a little, and had memorized quite a few Bible verses. On Sunday evenings he would often conduct a prayer meeting for his relatives and others. He had memorized a few old hymns, too, which they often sang with him leading, his arms gesturing in rhythm.

After crops were "laid by" (a phrase meaning no more tending until harvest), the men and older boys would get together a shotgun or two, some corn meal, coffee, bacon, lots of tobacco, knives, pails, a frying pan, and possibly an oil lantern. Thus outfitted, they would take to the hills and ridges for a week's expedition of digging ginseng. Their travels often took them into the more remote areas of Stone Mountain, where

the location of the prized ginseng was a carefully-guarded secret. They slept under cliffs and ledges, killed and ate small game, and generally "lived off the land." Jim, a brother-in-law of Jassie, his son, Benny, and a few other kinsmen often went together on these trips to the mountains.

I have read and heard much concerning the Melungeons' habits of making and drinking whiskey on Newman's Ridge. Those that were described in the above paragraphs were living in Lee County, Virginia, having moved there from the mining areas of Wise County. While the men were fond of whiskey, seldom refusing a drink, they never made or sold it, and few had enough money to buy it.

Old Josiah (known as an "old soldier") was allowed to vote under the "Grandfather Clause," in spite of his inability to decipher an election ballot, or even to register. This was also true of his sons, who (as I vaguely recall) were sometimes plied with "campaign liquor" on election day and persuaded to vote according to the wishes of some unscrupulous political boss.

We still had Melungeon families in our valley and on the surrounding ridges when I left the area in the middle 1920s. I remember a "Sam," whose color was darker than that of many mulattoes, but with different facial features. Mandy, his wife, had two older children who were also quite dark and kinky-haired. But a younger son was fair-skinned, a light brown, with curly hair and gray eyes. Their daughter, a second-grader at fourteen, weighed over a hundred pounds. Once she was accused of taking a trinket from a smaller classmate, and when I kept her in the room alone to question her about it, she stood up and yelled, in a deep, throaty voice:

"I'm goin' t'tell Pap on y'fer packin' t'on me a-stealin!"

Sam was an illiterate but diligent laborer. He finally managed to save enough money from his earnings to buy a small tract of land on the Ridge, where he spent the rest of his life among the plateaus and small clusters of his kinsmen.

I remember another man named Lem, who with his wife and numerous daughters occasionally came down to the crossroads market, either to a "gathering" or to visit relatives. None of this family were very dark, but some had high cheekbones, including Lem's wife. Around middle age, Lem decided to become a preacher, or at least a religious spokesman among his friends, relatives, and others who were interested in their type of worship. He frequently conducted services in his home, and attended meetings that were carried on by a Primitive Baptist denomination in the community.

One evening in the midst of a series of meetings, the members of a particular congregation had exhausted themselves singing songs like "Old Ship of Zion" and other familiar (to them) gospel songs. Even so, the presiding minister called upon his flock for "some good brother or sister to start another song." Over behind a big pot-bellied stove, a gaunt man with a scraggly mustache rose and began singing a "tune" that sounded familiar, but not in church. The melody was that of "Sourwood Mountain," an old folk song and "fiddle tune." However, the singer was using revised wordage that went something like this:

"There'll be no hypocrites in Heaven—
Hey-ho-diddle-dum-a-day!
We'll eat around the union table—
Hey-ho-diddle-dum-a-day!"

The vocalist was none other than Lem.

Our tenant, Jassie, once became quite ill with a severe attack of colitis. His family knew nothing of sanitation and seldom resorted to the services of a medical doctor. Our pastor's wife learned of his illness, and on a Sunday evening she and her husband stopped by my parents' house on their way to visit the ailing Jassie. On her arm, this lady (a Mrs. Warren) carried a soft white pillow and some food she had prepared for the patient. Eventually Jassie recovered from his illness, which would likely have been fatal to many of his white neighbors. As I have said previously, they were a hardy bunch.

The Warrens later moved to a little coal town in Wise County, Virginia. One day Mrs. Warren was at the company store buying some groceries when a gaunt man, covered from head to foot with coal dust, said to her:

"Y'r Miz War'n. Ain't ye'?"

She replied that she was.

"I don't guess y'know me, b't I'll never fergit th'time y'brung thet piller t'put 'nunder m'head w'en I wuz bad off w'th th'flux."

Jassie's sister, Delia, her husband Jim, Benny, Rhoeny, and their other children left our valley about the same time. They lived near each other in the Stone Mountain country. Delia was a dark, obese woman; Jim was quite the opposite, and might have served as a model for the cartoonist Chester Gould's *B. O. Plenty*. Both Jim and Benny were notorious gluttons. Once, in the 1930s, an area paper ran a story about Benny's unbelievable capacity for "food storage." It seems that a group had agreed to pay for all the food he could eat, which was: two whole fried chickens, a dozen boiled eggs, a loaf of bread, and a small watermelon.

As a lad, a joke Benny liked to tell concerned the time he took all his younger brothers and sisters into a dark hollow for a snipe hunt. He abandoned them, and they waited for hours for him to herd snipe into their paper bags (which they called "pokes").

Sam's daughter, Marindy, was the big girl of fourteen who protested so loudly when I asked about the accusation of theft made against her in school. She quit school as soon as she could and later married a farm tenant who was white. She was very dark, with dark eyes and drooping eyelids; however, her nose and mouth were more oriental than Caucasian or Ethiopian.

Marindy and her husband moved into the little shack where Jassie and Sary had lived more than twenty years previously. Several of their children were born there. As a rule, childbirth was a minor event with Melungeon women. The day that Marindy discovered she was in labor, she rushed outside and called to a neighbor on the opposite knoll, who in turn summoned my mother. Even though Mother had always been equal to any emergency, she found herself in an unprecedented situation. With neither a physician nor midwife available, the child was born before my mother reached the shack, with assistance only from the neighbor. By the time Marindy's husband arrived home from work that day, Marindy and her baby were sleeping comfortably, and my mother had wearily returned home. The young mother, likely as not, resumed her household chores the following morning.

Marindy had an uncle and aunt who lived over in the "Knob" area, whom I shall call Zeke and Hatty. Zeke was a big, ape-like man past middle age with typical Melungeon features. Neither he nor Hatty was very dark, but both had Oriental eyes. When it became known generally that Zeke had decided to leave Hatty and find a younger partner, someone asked Marindy why. She replied without hesitation:

"A-h, ah reckon he jist wanted t'change pasters."

When anyone inquired about the whereabouts of one of the tribe who was not on the scene, they almost invariably received the reply:

"I dunno. 'E went summers."

I spent the first year of my teaching career about three or four miles up the valley. The mother of two boys in my group was assisting a neighbor with her laundry just prior to the opening of school; the neighbor, a Mrs. Alderson, called the mother of my two Melungeon students "Sis." Mrs. Alderson asked Sis if the boys, Tom and Brisco, were going to school that year.

"I dunno," Sis said. "I've never hyerd'em say."

Then there was Jonas, a giant of a man physically; he came into the area just prior to the 1920s looking for a tenant house and farm work. He had yellowish skin, a broad, rather flat nose, dark brown, somewhat kinky hair, and brown eyes. Rumor had it that Jonas was part black, but the percentage was not known. He was very strong and took hard work in stride. He was also polite, loyal, and appeared to remain unruffled by any disturbing events around him. He usually spent his Sundays resting quietly at home, or strumming on his banjo, the only "luxury" he possessed.

Milly, his wife (who was, apparently, white) was just the opposite. She was quarrelsome and ill-natured, a disposition she seemed to have passed on to her children, even though some of them had Jonas's physical features.

Milly's disposition caused us to lose Jonas as a tenant on our farm. He was the most satisfactory worker we had had in many years, but she and her offspring got caught up in an unfortunate incident involving another tenant of ours, which went as follows:

Our greedy pigs invaded their vegetable garden, which no doubt was most irritating to them, since much of their food came from it. My mother sent our other tenant to remove the pigs and repair the fence, but as luck would have it, Jonas was absent. Milly and her daughter Ibby, a girl in her early teens, proceeded to "order him off" and called him vile names, to which our second tenant, Walt, replied with an equally wild "flow of strong language." Hearing him, Ibby seized a stone and

hurled it at Walt, and before he could duck it hit him on the forehead, making a deep cut. Walt left, going back to give my mother an account of the event while she treated and bandaged his wound.

We heard nothing from Jonas, Milly, or their children for a couple of days. Then, with the ill will of both their landlord and neighbor tenant hanging over their heads, Jonas and his family quietly packed up and moved their few belongings to another farm some miles away. Jonas later came and made a settlement with my father, and said nothing in defense of his belligerent family.

We had no news of Jonas for a year or two. Then one day our county paper carried the court indictments on the front page. To our suprise, we found Jonas's name among those who had been indicted at the recent term of court; he was charged with "Maiming." Apparently he had gone on a drunken spree and slashed another man's throat with a knife, barely missing the jugular. His victim recovered, but Jonas was sent to the penitentiary for a year or two.

That was how we learned that Jonas had always been considered dangerous when he was intoxicated.

# 1977

Much water has passed over the dam since 1969, when the first edition of this book saw print. Your author has received scores of letters, newspaper clippings, and photo-copied magazine articles on the subject. I have answered numerous queries, and have cooperated as much as I possibly could with others doing research on the Melungeons. In 1975 I even went to Sneedville, Tennessee, to see the outdoor drama *Walk Toward the Sunset*. It was well-written, the natural setting was fantastic, and the performance excellent.

Concerning the numerous letters I have received: I have not always been able to answer some of the questions put to me. One correspondent wished to know who the "Black Dutch" were; I have heard my elders refer to them ever since I can remember, but I doubt if a single one of them could have explained just who they were. My encyclopedia was useless, so I could only venture a guess. Perhaps they were descendants of those members of the Germanic races who were absorbed into the blood and culture of the Mediterranean people whom they, as the barbarians, conquered during the early centuries. It is my impression that the barbarians of the north were of fair complexion, as were the Scandinavians.

Later I received a query on the "Black Irish"; again I could only guess that they were (possibly) products of the Romans who followed St. Patrick on his mission to Christianize Ireland. Perhaps my readers can come up with authentic answers.

I also received a most interesting letter describing some "Black Indians." I have searched my files but have been unable to locate anything on them and am somewhat disappointed to be unable to give my readers any information.

In 1975 a lady from Tampa, Florida, wrote: "We have a similar situation in Florida with the Minorcans, and of course in the West there are the blue-eyed Mandan Indians. I don't imagine it will ever be definitely proved who they are and where they came from, but as far as the Melungeons are concerned, I lean toward the people who disappeared from the Lost Colony."

One native of Hancock County, Tennessee, says that he does not believe, after having lived in Texas most of his life and been in contact with persons of mixed white and Indian blood "in all degrees," that the original people known as Melungeons had as much Indian blood as some are inclined to believe. Of the mixtures of red, white, and black races, none had the features of the Newman's Ridge residents.

"They have some other kind of blood. In my opinion the original Melungeons that my ancestors found when they settled in what is now Hancock County, Tennessee, had no Negro blood whatsoever. But in the period before World War I about three mulattoes came to Blackwater and Newman's Ridge and took up with Melungeon women."

A native of Scott County, Virginia, who also lives in Texas, said of the so-called "Ramps":

"My father said they got the name Ramp from the fact that they were crazy about wild onions, and, many years ago when food was scarce, when the men were in the field or hunting, they would eat those onions wherever they could find them."

He added that the ramps were so potent that they contributed to a specific type of body odor.

"It is strong and hot. This sort of ties them to the Latin people, who are fond of onions, garlic, and red peppers."

Mr. William P. Grohse, who is not a native of the southern Appalachians but has spent many years in Hancock County, Tennessee, where he has been associated with the Vardy Mission of the Presbyterian Church, has written numerous articles for area publications. In a letter to me, he stated:

"Mahala Collins Mullins was a great aunt of my late wife. Her sister, Amelia, was the mother of my father-in-law, Logan Miser. She was the wife of Hamilton Miser (called "Ham"). Mahala's father was Solomon Collins; his wife was Jincie Goings, daughter of Joseph Goings and his wife, Millie Lovin. Solomon's father was also named Solomon.... Both Solomon, Sr. and Joseph Goings were Revolutionary War veterans. The name Goings was corrupted to Goin, Goine, Goins, Gwinn, etc.

"Vardy is named after my late wife's great-great-great grandfather, Vardy (or Vardiman) Collins, who held land grants for most of the land in the valley."

Mr. Grohse also said that Joseph Gibson of Hancock County served in the Confederate Army during the Civil War. Your author remembers Joe Gibson during his later years as an aged widower. He lived with his youngest son and his son's motherless children in Lee County, Virginia. This son married an attractive Caucasian girl.

## CONCLUSIONS

I will now try to answer the questions I enumerated in my introductory remarks at the beginning of these notes. Whether the answers are definitive enough is for you, my reader, to decide, but I do believe you will find some support for them on the previous pages.

Do the Melungeons have English ancestry? Are they in fact descended from the Lost Colony? It is reasonable almost beyond doubt that the

Melungeons had English ancestry. They were still speaking a form of Elizabethan English as recently as fifty years ago, and that form of our language is in use even now wherever Melungeon families cling together. Their English surnames supply further confirmation, although conclusive proof will probably always elude us.

Do the Melungeons have Indian ancestry? If so, what tribes? Perhaps the strongest evidence of their Indian ancestry is found in the written accounts of the English colonies at Roanoke Island. It is quite probable that these settlements had a few people who escaped the Indian massacres, the first of which was visited upon the remnants of Sir Richard Grenville's colony, the other upon Captain John White's colony. A few men in the Grenville group were unaccounted for when the English ships returned. These were all men, who, if any survived, would probably have married Indian or mixed-blood wives. It is possible that a few men, and probably one woman, escaped from the second massacre at Roanoke Island by going to live with friendly Indians who protected them (something, again, impossible to *prove*). These were the Croatoans, or so one would assume. According to historians, the Croatoans had some previous white admixture, which would likely have been Spanish or Portuguese.

Is there a connection with the "Lumbee" Indians? It is possible. The Lumbee Indians of Robeson County, North Carolina, spoke Elizabethan English, and may have been descendants of Sir Richard Grenville's colony, which traveled a more southerly course for refuge than did the colony of John White. The Lumbees were apparently a fusion of white blood and that of another Indian tribe to the southeast, which may have been the Cheraw or Creek tribe. However, their English blood in a sense suggests an indirect relationship with the tribe later called "Melungeon."

It is also possible that there is a relationship between the Melungeons and the Blue Ridge and Piedmont tribes (question 4), but the evidence is slight. Only once did we read of the claim of these tribes to Portuguese ancestry. They could have been extensions of the Maryland and Delaware groups, who, in some instances, also claim Portuguese ancestry.

Is there a Portuguese ancestry? As I see it, Portuguese ancestry is likely; all the older Melungeons have claimed it. It could only have occurred through contacts of shipwrecked Portuguese sailors and the Indians of the Carolinas who were friendly with the white colonists.

Miss Dromgoole's statement that "a Portuguese named Denham came to Newman's Ridge and married one of the Collins daughters" is possible, but it has no authenticity or foundation, other than the vague claims of the older Melungeons, who were illiterate and kept no written records. Their history and traditions were simply handed down from one generation to the next, and on occasion seem to have been confused with superstitious legends. Nevertheless, the Portuguese theory has been too long-standing and consistent to ignore.

It is unlikely that De Soto's party had any connection to the Melungeons, even though there has been a persistent tradition that De Soto did travel as far northward as Scott County, Virginia. But since De Soto was Spanish and died in 1542 (a quarter of a century before the first English colony arrived), it does not appear to have been an acceptable theory—that is, unless the Spanish descendants later mated with Indian-white mixtures from eastern North Carolina.

What role did the slaves play in the evolution of the Melungeons? Due to the caste system operating on them, many Melungeon groups have, at one time or another, been thrown into close contact with blacks, especially during the periods when Melungeons were forced to attend black schools and churches, and live close together. Another possibility is that during colonial warfare the Indians often killed white male settlers, taking their wives and daughters, as well as slaves, captive. In this way the three races could have mixed. However, in the case of the Melungeons, it does not likely go back that far.

The unusual endurance of the Melungeons to a hardy, outdoor existence may have come, at least in part, from their Indian ancestors. There are also indications that some of these qualities may have come from Portuguese and Moorish ancestors. Through lack of written history and the evident fusion of the races, only the Elizabethan English and white mode of dress have survived, with (possibly) some old English superstitions and ideas. Naturally, Melungeons have acquired many of the Indian customs that fit into their lives in the wilderness. Their dialects are still (mostly) old English.

Why is their history so vague? Why is it so difficult to give statistics? Their history is vague because of their lack of written records in the first place. Those with Indian ancestry have lost contact with their early forbears for the same reason. And those with Negro ancestry have done likewise.

As has been shown in previous chapters, there is no accuracy in names of races given in census and court records. Since Melungeons attended white schools, or Indian schools (or, now, integrated schools), there is no way of identifying who went where, or when, and thus no way of obtaining meaningful statistics. The opening of coal mines and other industries in southwestern Virginia, eastern Tennessee, and Kentucky has served to bring many of the Melungeons out of their mountain retreats seeking employment. Some have married whites and in many cases have lost their identity.

And finally, we have shown that the Melungeons have many kindred peoples scattered all over the landscape. They reside in Virginia, North and South Carolina, Georgia, and many other places. But like the Melungeons they too are dying out, going back the way they came, by intermarriage and assimilation, disappearing forever into the maelstrom that is called the great American melting pot.

## A Summary

Physical features of the Melungeons are indicative of much more than just an Indian-white mixture. While it is true that there are a few "traces" of black blood, there is even stronger evidence of an Old World background. This is especially noticeable in the women, many of whom have thin lips and "dreamy," Oriental-looking eyes. Small, graceful hands and feet are also significant.

Their aversion to formal education and the conventional restrictions of the white race, their "closeness" to nature, their physical endurance, skill in boating, primitive modes of fishing and hunting, as well as their knowledge of herbs, are likely carryovers from their Indian ancestors. Their efficiency in herding and handling livestock may be "inherited" from the Moors.

While some of their superstitious ideas may date back to their Indian forebears, it is also known that Anglo-Saxon pioneers of the southern Appalachians handed down innumerable traditions, legends, folklore, and the like to their descendants. Those who have retained most of their Anglo-Saxon heritage by remaining in the mountains still possess a wealth of that heritage in their old ballads, riddles, jingles, folk dances and games, and the "Jack Tales" so publicized by Richard Chase. They

also know how to tell numerous ghost stories. They carry with them good luck charms, consult the almanac for signs of the Zodiac, and plant crops in accordance with the phases of the moon. Their store of old signs and superstitions would fill a small book.

Snake-handling, which was described as one of their modern religious rites by Jesse Stuart, is not peculiar to the Melungeons; it is also practiced by other mountain religious sects. However, the Melungeons, with their knowledge of and attachment to nature, view the maligned reptile with much less antipathy than do their white neighbors, as a rule. (Perhaps those who use them in religious rituals base their beliefs on that portion of the Old Testament which reads, in part: "And Moses lifted up the serpent in the wilderness." This was apparently given as an example of faith for the purpose of healing.)

The proverbial shyness of many Melungeons may be due to their inability to express themselves in the conventional language of their more educated neighbors, and to their long years of withdrawal from other groups caused by the so-called "caste system."

There is no denying that the old English takes precedence in their speech and dialects.

They cannot be counted because they are not always identifiable. Sometimes it is easy to distinguish them from other whites by their outstanding physical features. Usually it is not too difficult to identify them when they live in groups by themselves. Even then, some are married to Caucasians, and it is through such intermarriages that many are lost in white blood.

# APPENDIX A

The information in this Appendix was taken from the 1830 census records of Hawkins and Grainger Counties in Tennessee. The (fc) means "free persons of color."

## Hawkins County, Tennessee - 1830
### (Heads of Families)

Fountain Goen (fc)
George Goen (fc)
John Goen (fc)
Betsy Goen (fc)
Zachariah Minor (fc)
Wiatt Collins (fc)
Andrew Collins (fc)
Martin Collins (fc)
John Collins (fc)
Martin Collins (fc)
Simeon Collins (fc)
Vardy Collins (fc)
Mary Collins (fc)
Levi Collins (fc)
Benjamin Collins (fc)
Edmund Collins (fc)
Betsy Jones (fc)
Edmund Goodman (fc)
James Moore (fc)
Dicey Bowling (fc)
Charles Beare (fc)
Timothy Williams (fc)

Harden Goen (fc)
Samuel Mullens (fc)
William Nichols (fc)
John Minor (fc)
Thomas Hale (fc)
Millenton Collins (fc)
James Collins (fc)
Charles Gibson (fc)
Esau Gibson (fc)
Cherod Gibson (fc)
Joseph F. Gibson (fc)
Andrew Gibson (fc)
Sheppard Gibson (fc)
Jordon Gibson (fc)
Polly Gibson (fc)
Jonathan Gibson (fc)
Jesse Gibson (fc)
Jordan Goodman (fc)
Burton Cold (fc)
Michael Bowling (fc)
Henry Mosely (fc)

## Grainger County, Tennessee - 1830
### (Heads of Families)

Edmund Bolen (fc)
Shadrach Bolen (fc)
Edmund Bolen (fc)

Ezekiel Bolen (fc)
Clabourn Bolen (fc)
Moses Collins (fc)

David Goan (fc)
John Goan (fc)
Thomas Goan (fc)
Nancy Goan (fc)
Preston Goan (fc)
Fanny Goan (fc)
Joseph Collins (fc)
Griffin Collins (fc)
Levi Collins (fc)

Gondly Collins (fc)
Dowell Collins (fc)
Lewis Collins (fc)
Encey Collins (fc)
Hardin Collins (fc)
Andrew Collins (fc)
Allen Collins (fc)
Lavinia Lafes (fc)

## APPENDIX B

The following information was taken from the 1860 census of Lee County, Virginia. Please note that Indians named Cole spelled it C-o-l-e (rather than C-o-a-l) in Harlan County, Kentucky, in both the 1860 and 1870 Census.

### Lee County, Virginia -1860 Census, Book I

| Name | Age | Born |
|------|-----|------|
| Page 44 | | |
| Family 204: | | |
| Isaac Coal | 58 | Wythe County VA |
| Isabella Coal | 62 | South Carolina |
| Matilda Coal | 1 | Claiborne County TN |
| | | |
| Family 313: | | |
| Solomon D. Hobs | 31 | Lee County VA |
| Sabina E. Hobs | 3 | Lee County VA |
| William C. Hobs | 3 | Lee County VA |
| Jefferson Coal | 15 | Lee County VA |
| Robert H. Hobs | 7 mo. | Lee County VA |
| | | |
| Family 342: | | |
| John Coal (Indian) | 61 | Lincoln County NC |
| Eliza Coal (Indian) | 18 | Scott County VA |
| Elizabeth Coal (Indian) | 15 | Knox County KY |
| Jacob Coal (Indian) | 2 | Lee County VA |
| Elmira Coal (Indian) | 1 | Lee County VA |
| | | |
| Family 343: | | |
| William Jones | 65 | Not given |
| William H. Lunsford | 8 | Carter County KY |
| Eliza Coal (Indian) | 26 | Lee County VA |
| Jane Coal (Indian) | 9 | Claiborne County TN |
| Elizabeth Coal (Indian) | 5 | Lee County VA |

Family 495:

| John A. Collins | 38 | Washington County VA |
|---|---|---|
| Mary Collins | 27 | Lee County VA |
| Samuel C. Collins | 5 | Lee County VA |
| Nancy J. Collins | 8 | Lee County VA |
| Henry F. Collins | 3 | Lee County VA |
| Elizabeth J. Collins | 1 mo. | Lee County Va |

Page 73

Family 565:

| Allen Milam | 60 | Tazwell County VA |
|---|---|---|
| Athi Milam | 61 | Lee County VA |
| July A. Vandepool | 24 | Lee County VA |
| John M. Coal (Indian) | 20 | Lee County VA |

Page 101

Family 778:

| David M. Coal | 34 | Clinton County KY |
|---|---|---|
| Jane Coal | 35 | Wythe County VA |
| Mary J. Coal | 16 | Smyth County VA |
| Alvira Coal | 13 | Smyth County VA |
| Robert Coal | 11 | Lee County VA |
| George Coal | 9 | Lee County VA |
| Member A. Coal | 3 | Lee County VA |
| Jas. N. Coal | 6 mo. | Lee County VA |

(There is a possibility that this family should not be considered Melungeon, since they came from an area where other "Coles" were not.)

Page 126

Family 968:

| Perry Collins | 30 | Claiborne County TN |
|---|---|---|

| Ann Collins | 30 | Claiborne County TN |
| Martha Collins | 10 | Claiborne County TN |
| Malissa Collins | 8 | Claiborne County TN |
| Blanton Collins | 6 | Claiborne County TN |
| Hazel Collins | 5 | Claiborne County TN |
| Litton Collins | 3 | Claiborne County TN |
| Sterlin Collins | 8 mo. | Claiborne County TN |

Page 133

Family 1024:
| David Collins | 27 | Hawkins County TN |
| Polly A. Collins | 22 | Scott County VA |
| John M. Collins | 2 | Lee County VA |

Page 134

Family 1028:
| William Collins | 23 | Lee County VA |
| Judy A. Collins | 29 | Lee County VA |
| Nace Collins | 10 | Lee County VA |
| Eliza Collins | 8 | Lee County VA |
| Nathaniel Collins | 7 | Lee County VA |
| Terrissa E. Collins | 3 | Lee County VA |
| Francis J. Collins | 1 mo. | Lee County VA |

Page 138

Family 1058:
| Henry Coal | 37 | Hancock County TN |
| Rebecca Coal | 38 | Hancock County TN |
| Elizabeth Coal | 8 | Claiborne County TN |
| William S. Coal | 3 | Hancock County TN |
| Adaline Singleton | 18 | Hancock County TN |
| Elen Singleton | 8 mo. | Hancock County TN |

Page 158

Family 1220:

| | | |
|---|---|---|
| Mary J. Coal | 35 | Lee County VA |
| John Coal | 14 | Lee County VA |
| Rachael A. Coal | 12 | Lee County VA |
| Mary Coal | 10 | Lee County VA |
| Martha Coal | 8 | Lee County VA |
| Reuben De Board | 20 | Russell County VA |
| Catharine De Board | 19 | Lee County VA |

The Scott County, Virginia, Census of 1850 also contained some relevant information, as follows:

(a) It included two Collins families, all of whom were born in Virginia.

(b) While there were evidently white families named Gibson living there, there were also ten Gibson families living in the same general area as the Melungeons. The heads of these families were born in Virginia, and none of them were past 45 years of age. One Gibson father was listed as having been born in "Penn.," which could easily have been "Tenn.," since the T and the P looked much alike in the old script. One head of family was born in North Carolina.

(c) Two Goins families were listed, one father born in Tennessee, the other in North Carolina.

(d) This census also listed a large family under the name of Ephriam Moore of Virginia (mentioned elswhere as a possible Melungeon family). These Moores are not to be confused with another family of Moores who lived near the Lee-Scott County line, and who owned slaves by that name.


## SOME SUGGESTED READING

The following list is *not* a bibliography of these notes. I have included it to provide those who have a deeper interest in the subject with the broadest possible range of information. Page numbers are given where they were available.

Addington, L.F. "Mountain Melungeons Let the World Go By." *Baltimore Sun,* Sunday, July 29, 1945, Section A, p. 3.

Armstrong, Zella. *Who Discovered America? The Amazing Story of Madoc.* Chattanooga: Lookout Publishing Company, 1950.

Aswell, James. "Lost Tribes of Tennessee's Mountains." *Nashville Banner,* August 22, 1937.

Aswell, James R. with E.E. Miller, et al. "God Bless the Devil!" *Liars Bench Tales,* Chapel Hill, 1940, pp. 207-243.

Babcock, William H. "The Nanticoke Indians of Indian River, Delaware." *The American Anthropologist,* Volume I, 1889, pp. 277-82.

Ball, Bonnie S. "America's Mysterious Race." *Read,* Volume 16, May, 1944, pp. 64-67.

_____ "Mystery Men of the Mountains." *Negro Digest,* Volume 3, January, 1945, pp. 39-41.

_____ "Virginia's Mystery Race." Virginia State Highway Bulletin, Volume 2, No. 6, April, 1945, pp. 2-3.

_____ "Who are the Melungeons?" *Southern Literary Messenger,* Volume 3, No. 2, June, 1945, pp. 5-7.

_____ "A Vanishing Race." *Mountain Life and Work,* Summer, 1960.

Barr, Phyllis. "The Melungeons of Newman's Ridge." Graduate thesis presented to the Department of English Faculty, East Tennessee State University, 1965.

Beale, Calvin. "American Triracial Isolates, Their Status and Pertinence to Genetic Research," *Eugenics Quarterly,* Volume 4, No. 4, December, 1957. American Eugenics Society, 230 Park Avenue, New York.

Beck, Henry C. "Fare to Midlands." *Forgotten Towns of Central New Jersey.* New York, 1939, pp. 73-89.

Bernstein, Carl. "Maryland's Brandywine People (We Sorts)." *Washington Post,* November 29, 1979.

Berry, Brewton. *Almost White.* New York: Macmillan Company, 1963.

Bible, Jean. "A People With an Unknown Past." *Baltimore Sunday Sun Magazine,* June 13, 1971.

_____ *The Melungeons of Yesterday and Today.* Dandridge, Tennessee, 1975.

Boland, Charles. *They All Discovered America.* New York: Doubleday,

Inc., 1961.

Brasch, Richard. *Mexico, a Country of Contrasts.* New York: David McKay Company, Inc., 1967.

Briggs, Olin. "Indians Have Tribe Proof." *The News Observer,* Tuesday, January 4, 1972.

Burnett, Swan M. "A Note on the Melungeons." *American Anthropologist,* Volume 2, October, 1889, pp. 347-49.

Caldwell, Joshua W. *Studies in the Constitutional History of Tennessee,* Second Edition, Cincinatti, 1907.

Cambaire, Celestin. *East Tennessee and Western Virginia Mountain Ballads.* London: Mitre Press, 1935.

*Century Dictionary and Encyclopedia.* New York, 1906. "Melungeon" defined, Volume 5, p. 3702.

*Constitution of Tennessee.* Annotated by Robert T. Shannon. Nashville: Tennessee Law Book Publishers, 1915.

Converse, Paul. "The Melungeons." *Southern Collegian,* December, 1912. Also, see the *Dictionary of American History,* Volume 3, New York, 1940.

Crawford, Bruce. "Letters to the Editor." *Coalfield Progress,* Norton, Virginia, July 11, 1940.

_____ "Hills of Home." *Southern Literary Messenger,* Volume 2, No. 5, May, 1940, pp. 302-313.

Dash, Joan. "Shepardim, A Modern Door to Fifteenth Century Spain." *Americas,* October, 1965.

Davis, Louise. "The Mystery of the Melungeons." *Nashville Tennessean Sunday Magazine,* September 22, 1963.

_____ "Are They Vanishing?" *Nashville Tennessean Sunday Magazine,* September 29, 1963.

Deacon, Richard. *Madoc and the Discovery of America.* New York: George Braziller, 1966.

"Delaware." *Encyclopedia Britannica,* Eleventh Edition, Volume 7, 1910-11, p. 948.

Dial, Adolph L. and David K. Eliades. "The Only Land I know." *A History of the Lumbee Indians,* 1975.

Donoghue, Frank L. "Tribal Reserve Broken By War." *New York Journal American,* Volume 2, March 24, 1942, pp. 1, 3, 5.

Driver, Harold. *The Americas on the Eve of Discovery.* Englewood Cliffs, New Jersey: Prentice Hall, 1964.

Dromgoole, Will Allen. "The Melungeons." *The Arena*, Volume 3, March, 1891, pp. 470-479.

＿＿＿＿＿ "The Melungeon Tree and Its Four Branches." *The Arena*, Volume 3, May, 1891, pp. 745-775.

Dunlap, A.R. and C.A. Westlager. "Trends in the Naming of Mixed-Blood Groups in the Eastern United States." *American Speech*, Volume 22, No. 2, April, 1947, pp. 81-87.

"East Tennessee Historical Society Bulletin," No. 32, 1960.

Editorial: "Drama of the Melungeons." *Grit*. Family Section, June 27, 1971.

Editorial: "The Last of the Melungeons." Focus, *Kinsport Times-News*, Sept. 5, 1971.

Estabrook, A.H. and E.E. McDougle. *Mongrel Virginians*. Baltimore: The Williams and Williams Company, 1926.

Faulkner, Charles. *The Old Stone Fort*. Knoxville: The University of Tennessee Press, 1968.

Federal Writers Guide. *Tennessee, a Guide to the State*. New York: Viking Press, 1939, p. 362.

Fell, Barry. "America B.C." *Quadrangle*. New York: The New York Times Book Company, 1976.

Fetterman, John. "The Melungeons." *Louisville Courier-Journal and Times Magazine*, Sunday, March 30, 1969.

＿＿＿＿＿ "The Mystery of Newman's Ridge." *Life* Magazine, June 26, 1970. (Not in all editions.)

Fisher, George P. "The So-Called Moors of Delaware." *Milford Herald*, Milford, Delaware, June 15, 1985.

Foster, Lawrence. "Negro-Indian Relationships in the Southeast." Philadelphia: University of Pennsylvania Press, 1935.

Frady, Gloria. "She Went Into the Hills to Do What Was Needed." *The State*, Columbia, South Carolina, February 3, 1974.

Franklin, Ben A. "Indians Resist Integration Plan in NC County." *The New York Times*, September 13, 1970.

Frazier, E. Franklin. *The Negro Family in the United States*. Chicago, 1940, pp. 226-29.

＿＿＿＿＿ "The Jackson Whites." *Eugenical News*, Volume XVI, No. 12, December, 1931, p. 218.

＿＿＿＿＿ "Native Sons." In Letters to *Time*, Volume 2, No. 15, July 22, 1935, pp. 1-2.

_____ "The Negro in New Jersey." Report of a survey by the Interracial Committee of New Jersey Conference in Social Work in cooperation with the State Department of Institutions and Agencies, December, 1932.

Gaillard, Frye. "The Lumbees Fight Back: A Struggle For Identity." *Raleigh News and Observer,* July 11, 1971.

Gamble, John. "Melungeon Line Almost Extinct." *Kingsport Times-News,* Kingsport, Tennessee, Thursday, November 26, 1964.

General Article: "Melungeon Line Goes On Despite Money Problem." *Kingsport Times-News,* April 19, 1972.

Gilbert, William H. Memorandum concerning the characteristics of the larger mixed-blood "racial islands" in the Eastern United States. *Social Forces,* Volume 21, No. 4, May, 1946, pp. 438-447.

_____ "Surviving Indian Groups," "Racial Islands," and other pamphlets. Government and General Research Division, Library of Congress, Washington.

Glen, Juanita. "Hancock Countians Prepare for Drama." *Knoxville Journal,* Thursday, May 1, 1969.

Goodspeed. *History of Tennessee* (East Tennessee Edition). Chicago and Nashville: The Goodspeed Publishing Company, 1887.

Gordon, Cyrus H. "Theory That Melungeons Came From Jewish Origin." *Argosy Magazine,* January, 1971.

Governors and Councillors of Virginia. *A True and Sincere Declaration, 1609.* Library of Congress.

Grant, Sandra. "They Work Here, But Their Ties Are Elsewhere." *Baltimore Evening Sun,* September 28, 1970.

Grohse, William. "The Land of Mystery." *Hancock County Post,* July 2, 1970.

_____ "The Old Solomon Collins Homestead." *Powell Valley News,* Pennington Gap, Virginia, Thursday, April 8, 1976.

Hale, W.T. and D.L. Meritt. *A History of Tennessee and Tennesseans.* Volume 1. Chicago and New York: Lewis Publishing Company, 1913.

Hamer, Philip L. *Roman Survival.* Chillicothe, Ohio: The Ross County Historical Society, 1960.

Hakluyt Society. *The Roanoke Voyagers,* Volume 2. Library of Congress.

Haun, Mildred. *The Hawk's Done Gone.* Edited by Herschel Grower. Nashville: Vanderbilt University Press, 1968.

Head. *Tennessee Supreme Court Reports,* Volume 3, 1858.

*Heads of Families-North Carolina.* Spartanburg: The Reprint Company, 1961.

Heiskell, Eliza N. "Strange People of East Tennessee." *Arkansas Gazette,* Little Rock, January 14, 1912.

Henderson, Harry and Tom Shaw. "Smokey Mountain Boy." *Colliers,* November 11, 1944.

Humphrey. *Tennessee Supreme Court Reports,* Volume 1, 1839, Volume 2, 1848.

Hunter, Kermit. *Walk Toward the Sunset.* Outdoor drama about the Melungeons staged at Sneedville, Tennessee, since 1969.

*Indians of North Carolina.* Senate Document No. 677, 1915, Library of Congress.

Ivey, Saundra Keyes. "Aunt Mahala Mullins in Folklore, Fakelore, and Other Literature." *Tennessee Folklore Society Bulletin.* Volume XLI, No. 1, March, 1975.

*Journal of the Convention of the State of Tennessee Convened for the Purpose of Amending the Constitution thereof.* Nashville, Tennessee, 1834, pp. 88-89.

King, Lucy. "The Melungeons." *The Boston Traveler,* April 13, 1889, p. 6.

Lear, John. "Ancient Landings in America." *Saturday Review of Literature,* July 18, 1970, pp. 18, 19, 34.

Lewis, Thomas and Madeline Kneberg. *Tribes that Slumber: Indians of the Tennessee Region.* Knoxville: University of Tennessee Press, 1966.

Mahan, A.T. *Admiral Farragut.* Great Commanders series. New York: D. Appleton & Company, 1892.

McGee, G.R. *History of Tennessee.* New York: American Book Company, 1911.

McMillan, Hamilton. "Sir Walter Raleigh's Lost Colony." Senate Document No. 677, 1915, Library of Congress.

Meigs. *Tennessee Supreme Court Reports,* Volume 1, 1832.

Moore, J.T. and A.P. Foster, editors. *Tennessee, the Volunteer State, 1769-1923.* Chicago, Volume 1, 1923. See pp. 790-91.

Morison, Samuel Eliot. *The European Discovery of America: The Northern Voyages, A.D. 500-1600.* New York: The Oxford University Press, 1971.

Mullen, Robert. *The Latter-Day Saints: The Mormons, Yesterday and Today.* New York: Doubleday, 1966.

Mynders, A.D. "Next to News." *Chattanooga Times,* June 17, 1945. Section 2, p. 10, column 3.

New York Times News Service. "Melungeon Colony Fading Away." *Chicago Tribune,* August 19, 1971.

Nordheimer, Jon. "Mysterious Hill Folk Vanishing." *New York Times,* Tuesday, August 10, 1971.

*North Carolinian, The.* Volume 1. Raleigh: Department of Archives and History, 1955-56.

Osborne, Hampton. "Mysterious People." In "Echoes of the Hills," a column published in the *Cumberland Times,* Clintwood, Virginia, June 4, 1956.

Pollitzer, William and William H. Brown. "Survey of Demography, Anthropometry, and Genetics in the Melungeons of Tennessee: An Isolate of Hybrid Origin in Process of Dissolution." Department of Anthropology, University of North Carolina, Chapel Hill. *Human Biology,* Volume 41, 1969.

Pollitzer, William. "The Physical Anthropology and Genetics of Marginal People of the Southeastern United States." *American Anthropologist,* Volume 74, No. 3, 1972.

Price, Edward T. "The Melungeons: A Mixed-Blood Strain of the Southern Appalachians." *The Geographical Review,* Volume 41, No. 2, April, 1951.

_____ "A Geographic Analysis of White-Negro-Indian Racial Mixtures in the Eastern United States." *Annals of the Association of American Geographers,* Volume XLIII, June, 1953, No. 2.

Price, Henry. *Melungeons: The Vanishing Colony of Newman's Ridge.* 26 pages. Sold by the Hancock County Drama Association, Box 95, Sneedville, Tennessee 37869.

Price, Prentiss. *Tennessee Marriage Records.* Volume 2. Knoxville: Clinchdale Press, 1958.

Ramsey, J.G.M. *Annals of Tennessee to the End of the Eighteenth Century.* Charleston, 1953.

Rawlins, Bill. "East Tennessee Melungeons Have A Past Clouded in Myth." *Knoxville News-Sentinel,* October 10, 1958.

*Report on Indians Taxed and Indians not Taxed in the United States at the 11th Census, 1890.* Washington: Department of the Interior, Census Office, 1894, p. 391.

Rothrock, Mary. *The French Broad-Holston Country.* Knoxville: The Knox County History, East Tennessee Historical Society, 1946.

Sams, Conway Whittle. *Conquest of Virginia.* Washington: Library of Congress, 1924.

Sevier Letter. Chicago: Newberry Library, E.E. Ayers Collection.

Shepherd, Lewis. *Memoirs of Judge Lewis Shepherd.* Chattanooga, 1915.

Smith, John (Captain). *True Relations.* Library of Congress.

Smithsonian Institution Annual Report for 1948. Washington: Government Printing Office, 1949, pp. 407-438.

Sneed. *Tennessee Supreme Court Reports.* Volume 3, 1856.

Speck, Frank G. "The Jackson Whites." *The Southern Workman,* February, 1911, pp. 104-107.

_____ "The Nanticoke Community of Delaware." *Heye Foundation Contributions from the Museum of the American Indian,* Volume 2, No. 4, New York, 1915.

Storms, J.C. "Origin of the Jackson Whites of the Ramapo Mountains." Manuscript, Park Ridge, New Jersey, 1936.

Stuart, Jesse. *Daughter of Legend.* New York: McGraw-Hill, 1965.

Swital, Chet. "In the Ramapos." Letters to *Time,* Volume 2, No. 15, July 22, 1935, pp. 1-2.

Terhune, Albert Payson. "Twelve-Toes Races of People Bred In North Jersey's 'Lost Colony'." *Philadelphia Record,* June 6, 1940, p. 1.

United States Census Reports of Virginia and Tennessee, 1830, 1850, 1860.

United States Federal Writers' Project. *New Jersey: Bergen County Panorama.* Hackensack, New Jersey, 1940, pp. 179-180, 305.

_____ *New Jersey, a Guide to Present and Past.* New York, 1939, pp. 124 and 505.

Walraven, O.N. *The Melungeons of Oakdale.* Manuscript No. G.08 from the WPA Federal Writers' guide, filed in McClung Historical Collection, Lawson McGhee Library, Knoxville, Tennessee.

Weeks, S.B. "Lost Colony of Roanoke." *Papers of the American Historical Association,* Volume 5, 1891. See the footnote, pp. 132-33.

Weslager, C.A. *Delaware's Forgotten Folk.* New York, 1943.

Williams, Samuel C. *Dawn of the Tennessee Valley and Tennessee History.* Johnson City: The Watauga Press, 1937.

_____ *Early Travels in the Tennessee Country.* Johnson City: The Watauga Press, 1928.

_____ *Adair's History of American Indians.* Edited. Johnson City: The Watauga Press, 1930.

Wilson, Goodridge. "The Southwest Corner." *Roanoke Times,* February 25, 1934.

Wooten, James T. "A Look at the Haliwa Indians." New York Times News Service, Daytona Beach *Sunday News Journal,* August 13, 1972.

Worden, W.L. "Sons of the Legend." *Saturday Evening Post,* October 18, 1947.

Yarbrough, Willard. "Maligned Mountain Folk May Be Topic of Drama." *Knoxville News-Sentinel,* January 8, 1968.

_____ "Melungeon Ways Are Passing." *Knoxville News-Sentinel,* April 26, 1972.

Zachary, Thomas. "The Melungeons." Undergraduate thesis, Department of Education, University of Tennessee.

Zuber, Leo. "The Melungeons." Manuscript No. G.08 from the WPA Federal Writers Guide, filed in McClund Historical Collection, Lawson McGhee Library, Knoxville.